AN UNOFFICIAL ENCYCLOPEDIA OF STRATEGY FOR FORTNITERS

A GUIDE TO SKINS, TOOLS, GEAR, AND ACCESSORIES

JASON R. RICH

Sky Pony Press
New York

Copyright © 2019 by Hollan Publishing, Inc.

Fortnite® is a registered trademark of Epic Games, Inc.

The Fortnite game is copyright © Epic Games, Inc.

Sky Pony Press books may be purchased in bulk at special discounts for sales promotion, corporate gifts, fund-raising, or educational purposes. Special editions can also be created to specifications. For details, contact the Special Sales Department, Sky Pony Press, 307 West 36th Street, 11th Floor, New York, NY 10018 or info@skyhorsepublishing.com.

Sky Pony® is a registered trademark of Skyhorse Publishing, Inc.®, a Delaware corporation.

Visit our website at www.skyponypress.com.

10 9 8 7 6 5 4 3 2 1

Library of Congress Cataloging-in-Publication Data is available on file.

Series design by Brian Peterson

Hardcover ISBN: 978-1-5107-4460-8
E-book ISBN: 978-1-5107-4468-4

Printed in China

TABLE OF CONTENTS

SECTION 1

PREPARE TO EXPERIENCE
FORTNITE: BATTLE ROYALE

When *Fortnite: Battle Royale* was first released in late September 2017, it quickly became so much more than just another multi-player, combat-oriented adventure game.

Now, with more than 125 million active players experiencing the game on their PC, Mac, PlayStation 4, Xbox One, Nintendo Switch, Apple iPhone, Apple iPad, or Android-based mobile device, *Fortnite: Battle Royale* is nothing short of a global phenomenon!

Many of the screenshots featured within this unofficial strategy guide were taken on a PlayStation 4 using *Fortnite: Battle Royale's* Playground mode. Depending on which game play mode you choose, and which gaming system you're using, the location where game-related information is displayed will vary.

There are numerous reasons why *Fortnite: Battle Royale* has become so popular, one of which is that it allows gamers to showcase their personality and attitude—not just their gaming skills. Epic Games continues to release new ways for players to customize the appearance of their character, plus showcase personality and attitude using three types of emotes, including many different dance moves (one of which is shown here).

Spray paint tags allow gamers to use virtual spray paint to add colorful graffiti to any flat surface on the island. Shown here, several different spray paint tag designs were used on the country club sign in front of the main clubhouse at Lazy Links.

Tossing graphic icons into the air is another way gamers can express themselves during a match. Some gamers use emotes as an in-game greeting. Others use them to gloat after defeating an enemy, or as a way to release some tension after an intense firefight. How and when you use emotes is entirely up to you.

No matter which game play mode you choose to experience—Solo, Duos, Squads, or a 50 v 50 match, for example—anytime you visit the mysterious island where each and every match takes place, not only does each soldier react differently (because each is being controlled in real time by a different gamer), but each of the 100 soldiers tends to look unique.

Additional limited-edition outfits and accessories get unlocked within the game by completing Battle Pass challenges. In fact, just by purchasing a new Battle Pass, you're guaranteed to receive several exclusive outfits. At the start of each new gaming season (approximately every three months), a new Battle Pass is released and the previous one expires.

Decide whether to purchase just the Battle Pass or spend a bit more and immediately unlock 25 Battle Pass tiers by purchasing a Battle Pass Bundle.

Every day within *Fortnite: Battle Royale*'s Item Shop, a different selection of outfits, accessories, and emotes are released. These give gamers who are willing to spend some money limitless customization possibilities when it comes to choosing a look for their soldier.

Shown here are two of the outfits that could be unlocked immediately upon purchasing the Season 5 Battle Pass Bundle (which included the Battle Pass for Season 5, as well as the ability to immediately unlock the first 25 Battle Pass tiers without completing any challenges). With this option, the Huntress and Drift outfits immediately became available to gamers.

Many outfits are released in conjunction with matching accessories. These are referred to as sets. Shown here, Ravage is about to be purchased for 2,000 V-Bucks (which equates to approximately $20.00 US). This outfit is part of the Nevermore set. The Ravage outfit includes a matching back bling (backpack) and contrail design. The optional pickaxe design and glider design for the Nevermore set are sold separately. Some outfits come bundled with matching back bling, but others do not.

Twitch Prime Packs are another source for exclusive, limited-edition outfits and accessory items. New Twitch Prime Packs are released every few months. To acquire one, you'll need to be a paid Amazon Prime subscriber and set up a free Twitch.tv account. For more information about Twitch Prime Packs, visit https://help.twitch.tv/customer/en/portal/articles/2572060-twitch-prime-guide.

Once outfits are acquired, further customization is possible by choosing a separate back bling (backpack) design, pickaxe design (shown here), glider design, and contrail design for a soldier. For some outfits, additional Style variations can be unlocked by completing challenges.

A contrail design is the animation that's displayed bursting from a soldier's hands (and sometimes their feet as well) during their free fall from the Battle Bus at the start of a match. Typically, contrail designs must be unlocked by completing Battle Pass challenges or free challenges. Some come with Twitch Prime Packs, but these typically are not sold by the Item Shop, and contrails seldom come bundled with outfits.

Simply by visiting the Locker prior to a match, you're able to choose an outfit (along with accessory items) that can make your soldier look sinister, powerful, mysterious, or whimsical, based on your mood and gaming strategy. The possibilities are endless!

A Few Things to Think About When Choosing an Outfit

Part of the fun is mixing and matching outfits with accessory items from different sets in order to make your soldier look truly unique. Shown here, the Overtaker outfit (which is part of the Vanishing Point set) was combined with the Boombox back bling (part of the Spandex Squad set) and the Balloon Axe pickaxe design (which is part of the Party Paradise set).

If you want your enemies to fear you, choose an outfit like Raven or Oblivion that shows you mean business.

Since unique outfits are released in conjunction with some in-game events, as well as real-world holidays, you can show your festive side by dressing your soldier up for that special occasion. This Magnus outfit was released at the start of Season 5, when Epic Games added the Viking village as an unlabeled point of interest on the island map. At least throughout Season 5, this area could be found at map coordinates B5.5, although it could be replaced or revamped in future seasons.

This Fireworks Team Leader outfit is another example of a holiday-themed outfit that was offered for a limited time around the Independence Day July Fourth holiday in the United States.

Some outfits are brightly colored and/or oversized. Sure, these look amazing, but they'll also make your soldier an easier target to spot on the island. To lower your chances of getting defeated, consider choosing an outfit that allows your soldier to blend in and not stand out during intense battles.

If you come across an adversary whose soldier is dressed in the Tomatohead outfit, but the outfit includes the Tomatohead Crown, this means you're dealing with an experienced player who was able to unlock this outfit style by completing a series of rather difficult challenges. In other words, if you see the Tomatohead Crown being worn by an enemy also dressed in the Tomatohead outfit, it's probably best to avoid that soldier. He's definitely being controlled by a skilled gamer.

Anytime you're playing a Duos or Squads match, for example, it's essential that you and your partner, or you and your squad mates, communicate throughout each match in order to plan and execute perfectly timed and well-coordinated attacks. To show your competition that you really mean business, consider choosing matching outfits with your partner or squad mates. Each gamer can then customize their own soldier's appearance by adding a different pickaxe and/or back bling design.

The most experienced gamers who play *Fortnite: Battle Royale* are able to unlock exclusive outfits and accessory items that can't be purchased from the Item Shop. Anytime you see a soldier wearing one of these outfits, such as Sun Strider (which could be unlocked by completing tier 47 during Season 5), you know the gamer controlling that soldier is highly skilled and will likely be extremely

difficult to defeat. Alternatively, those gamers paid a lot of extra money to unlock a bunch of Battle Pass tiers, and they're basically posers.

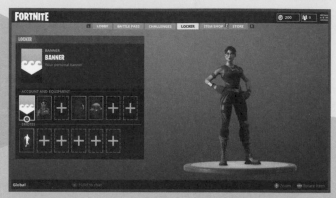

If you're one of those top-ranked and experienced gamers, but you don't want to tip off your competition, consider dressing your soldier up in one of the default outfits, like Jungle Scout, that are provided for free when a new gamer starts playing *Fortnite: Battle Royale*. If your competition thinks you're a noob, their guard will go down, likely making them easier to defeat.

Customizing Your Soldier's Appearance Is Totally Optional

Fortnite: Battle Royale costs nothing to play. That's right, it's 100 percent free! Anyone can download and install the game, set up a free Epic Games account, and start experiencing the game using the default outfit provided to their soldier.

To acquire outfits and accessory items, whether they're purchased from the Item Shop or unlocked by completing Battle Pass challenges, costs money. It's necessary to purchase a new Battle Pass at the start of each gaming season, which is approximately every three months.

By completing certain Battle Pass challenges, you can unlock exclusive outfits and accessories, as well as additional outfit styles (for certain outfits). Shown here is the Conquest glider, which was unlocked upon completing tier 39 of the Season 5 Battle Pass. This glider is part of the Norse (Viking-themed) set. To learn more about Battle Passes, visit www.epicgames.com/fortnite/en-US/battle-pass.

No matter how much money you spend on outfits and accessory items, these are all for cosmetic purposes only. None give your soldier any competitive advantage whatsoever. You can spend upwards of $20.00 for a limited-edition "Legendary" outfit, such as this Rex outfit and back bling bundle (which will make your soldier look totally lit), and then spend more money on a fancy pickaxe design, backpack design, and glider design, but no outfit or optional accessory items will make your soldier stronger, faster, or more powerful.

Despite offering hundreds of different pickaxe designs, they all function exactly the same way, although each design looks totally different.

Every so often, Epic Games offers a Starter Pack, which includes an exclusive outfit, matching back bling, and 600 V-Bucks for $4.99. When this offer is available, it's featured within the Store (where V-Bucks are purchased), not from the Item Shop.

Regardless of which glider design you use in conjunction with your soldier, they all function exactly the same when it comes to functionality, navigational control, and speed, for example.

Everything you purchase from the Item Shop, along with all of the items you unlock or acquire, become yours to keep. They get stored within the Locker, which is permanently tied to your Epic Games account. Your V-Bucks balance is also tied to your Epic Games account.

In order to make in-game purchases, you'll first need to visit the Store and use real money to acquire V-Bucks (in-game currency). As you can see here, V-Bucks are sold in bundles. The more V-Bucks you buy at once, the bigger discount you receive. All in-game purchases are optional, however.

It's important that you never reveal your account password to anyone, especially other gamers you're playing with during a Duos, Squads, or 50 v 50 match, for example. To help protect your Epic Games account, it's a good idea to turn on the optional Two-Factor Authentication feature. For more information about this feature, visit www.Fornite.com/2FA.

Get Ready for an Awesome Gaming Experience

During each *Fortnite: Battle Royale* match you experience, you'll need to juggle a wide range of tasks and do whatever becomes necessary to stay alive and become the last person standing in order to achieve #1 Victory Royale.

To be successful, you'll need to safely explore the island; become a fast and masterful builder; develop strategies for avoiding the deadly storm; collect and harvest resources (wood, stone, and metal); build up an arsenal (composed of a handpicked selection of weapons and loot items); and then engage in intense firefights and battles. One particularly fun way to explore the island is to drive an All Terrain Kart (ATK). These can be taken almost anywhere on the island and allow you to get around quickly.

Don't be fooled! Becoming a highly skilled *Fortnite: Battle Royale* player will take a lot of practice! Just because you choose an outfit that makes your soldier look tough or menacing, this does not magically make you capable of winning matches!

Whether or not you're able to survive on the island will depend on your gaming skills, reflexes, timing, how well you utilize the weapons at your soldier's disposal, and your knowledge of the island. How well you fight and juggle your responsibilities during a match will determine whether you get defeated or achieve #1 Victory Royale.

Because you're experiencing each match in conjunction with up to 99 other gamers—each controlling their own soldiers in real time—you'll need to contend with each of the unique strategies these gamers choose to utilize. The actions of other gamers, combined with the random movement of the deadly storm, ensures that each and every match you experience (regardless of the game play mode you choose) will be different.

You Can Look Good While Defeating Enemies

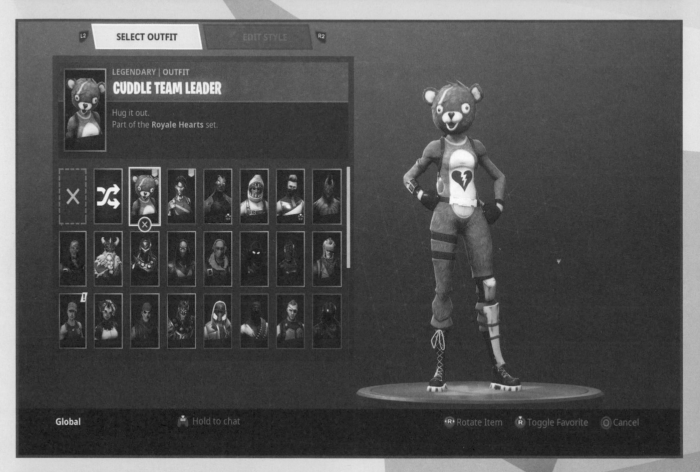

The outfits are showcased in alphabetical order within Section 3—An "A" to "Z" Guide to 50 Awesome *Fortnite: Battle Royale* Outfits. Some outfits, like Cuddle Team Leader and Tomatohead, have become iconic and instantly identifiable with *Fortnite: Battle Royale*.

As you learn about each outfit and the matching back bling designs, pickaxe designs, glider designs, and contrail designs available for them, you'll also discover proven tips and strategies that'll help make you a better *Fortnite: Battle Royale* player, regardless of your soldier's appearance.

The main focus of this unofficial strategy guide is to showcase more than 50 of the hundreds of unique outfits that Epic Games continues to make available and to help you choose the best outfits and accessory items (sets) when customizing the appearance of your soldier.

SECTION 2

CUSTOMIZE YOUR SOLDIER'S APPEARANCE WITH OUTFITS AND ACCESSORY ITEMS

Aside from the intense and challenging gaming experience offered by *Fortnite: Battle Royale*, one of the most popular features has turned out to be a gamer's ability to customize the appearance of his or her soldier. Once again, no matter how lit your soldier looks, the optional outfits and accessory items provide no competitive advantage whatsoever. They're for cosmetic purposes only. Plus, the majority of outfits and accessories cost money.

Ways to Acquire Outfits and Accessory Items

There are several ways to obtain new outfits for your soldier. These include:

- Purchasing them from the Item Shop
- Unlocking them by completing certain Battle Pass tiers
- Acquiring them as part of a Twitch Prime Pack
- Purchasing a Starter Pack from the Store (where V-Bucks are purchased)
- Receiving or unlocking an outfit that's part of a special promotion

Make Purchases from the Item Shop

From the Lobby, select the Item Shop tab that's displayed near the top-center of the screen, and each day, you'll discover a new selection of outfits, accessory items, and emotes available for sale. The prices for these items are listed in V-Bucks.

V-Bucks are in-game currency that must be acquired in bundles from the Store. They cost real money. By completing certain Battle Pass challenges, you can also unlock small bundles of V-Bucks, but what you're able to unlock won't allow you to afford the rare and limited-edition items offered by the Item Shop. Plus, to participate in Battle Pass challenges, you'll need to purchase the current gaming season's Battle Pass.

V-Bucks can only be purchased from within the *Fortnite: Battle Royale* game using a credit card, debit card, or PayPal.

Depending on which gaming system you're using, the actual in-game purchases you make (for V-Bucks) will be conducted through the PlayStation Store if you're a PS4 gamer (shown here), the Nintendo eShop if you're a Nintendo Switch gamer, the Xbox Live Gold store if you're an Xbox One gamer, or the App Store if you're playing on an iPhone or iPad. For all other gaming systems, Epic Games handles the online transactions. If you're offered V-Bucks from any other source, it's likely a scam!

How Much Outfits Cost

An outfit's category simply relates to how often it's rereleased within the Item Shop. An Uncommon Outfit is the least expensive and will be made available within the Item Shop often. However, Epic or Legendary outfits are considered limited edition. These are offered for a very limited time (typically between 24 and 48 hours) and may never be rereleased. If they are made available again, it'll be after months or years.

Notice the red and white "Pick Your Style" banner that's displayed in conjunction with the Hime outfit. This indicates that multiple versions of that outfit are available. In this case, Hime is the female version and Musha is the male version of the outfit in this set.

As you browse the Item Shop each day, you'll discover outfits range in price from 800 V-Bucks (approximately $8.00 US) to 2,000 V-Bucks (approximately $20.00 US).

Remember, while outfits are categorized as "Uncommon," "Rare," "Epic," or "Legendary," an outfit's rating has nothing do to with its strength or capabilities. All outfits (and accessory items) function exactly the same way and provide no additional speed, strength, agility, capabilities, or special powers to your soldier.

Each category of outfit is priced differently:

- Uncommon (Green) Outfits—800 V-Bucks
- Rare (Blue) Outfits—1,200 V-Bucks
- Epic (Purple) Outfits—1,500 V-Bucks
- Legendary (Gold)—2,000 V-Bucks

Some more expensive outfits come bundled with additional items, such as matching back bling and, once in a while, a matching contrail design. This Musha outfit is considered Legendary. It comes with matching back bling and is priced at 2,000 V-Bucks.

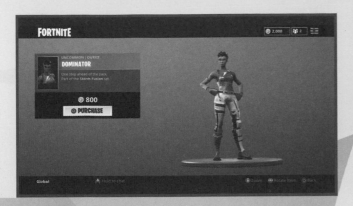

The less expensive outfits, like this Uncommon Dominator outfit, come with just the outfit and no accessory items. When outfits are bundled with accessory items, they're sold together for one price, but appear within your Locker as separate items. For example, the outfit will be placed in the Locker with your other outfits, and the matching back bling will be placed with your other back bling designs in a separate section of the Locker.

The price for each of these items will typically be between 500 V-Bucks and 1,500 V-Bucks each (which equates to between $5.00 US and $15.00 US). When you buy larger bundles of V-Bucks, you receive a discount, which makes these purchases a little less costly.

Make sure you know how much real money you're actually spending when making in-game purchases. To acquire a single entire Legendary set, which includes an outfit, along with a matching back bling, pickaxe, and glider design, for example, it could cost you upwards of $30.00 (US) to $50.00 (US) . . . Yikes!

At the same time a new outfit is introduced, sometimes matching accessories are made available, but sold separately. When multiple matching items are available, they're part of a set that will have a name. For example, Musha is part of the Bushido set. The optional accessories might include a matching pickaxe design and glider design.

complete the challenges associated with each Battle Pass tier.

A typical Battle Pass includes at least 100 tiers. Each time you complete the challenges associated with one tier, a new prize item is unlocked. Prizes can include an outfit, accessory item, contrail design, or small bundle of V-Bucks. Each Battle Pass includes at least several unique outfits—some of which can only be acquired by completing the challenges associated with the Battle Pass.

Each time you visit the Item Shop, you can purchase as many items as you wish, but one at a time (as long as you have enough V-Bucks linked with your account). Once you make a purchase and then see the "Successfully Purchased" screen appear, this means you now own that item. It automatically gets stored within the appropriate section of your Locker.

Complete Battle Pass Challenges

Another popular way to acquire exclusive outfits that are typically not available elsewhere is to purchase a Battle Pass each gaming season (approximately every three months) and

To participate in these challenges you'll need to purchase the Battle Pass. To do this, from the Lobby, click on the Battle Pass tab that's displayed near the top of the screen. At the start of a new season, a new Battle Pass is released and the previous one expires. However, all prizes you unlock during a gaming season are yours to keep. Each outfit and accessory item gets stored within the Locker, and other prizes get linked with your account.

If you purchase a Battle Pass, but don't want to complete certain challenges in order to unlock the prizes, for 150 V-Bucks each, you can pay to have one tier at a time unlocked. For example, by purchasing Tier 91 during Season 5, this Fancy Basketball specialty emote was unlocked.

Twitch Prime Packs

For gamers who are paid subscribers to Amazon Prime and who set up a free Twitch. tv account, every few months, a new Twitch Prime Pack is released. When you redeem a Twitch Prime Pack, it includes at least one exclusive outfit along with accessory items and a few emotes.

Promotional Outfits

At least once per season, Epic Games offers an exclusive outfit (sometimes with matching accessories) as part of a Starter Pack promotion. For example, from the Store, this promotion included the Wingman outfit with matching back bling along with a bundle of 600 V-Bucks for $4.99 (US).

The Ace outfit was also originally offered as part of a Starter Pack promotion exclusively from the Store (not the Item Shop). For $4.99 (US), the outfit was bundled with the matching Swag Bag back bling design, along with 600 V-Bucks.

The Ace outfit is part of the Getaway Gang set.

Unlock Styles for Certain Outfits

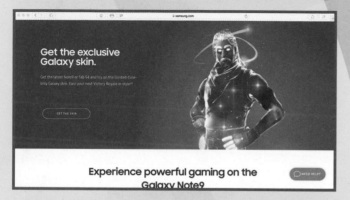

When Epic Games released the Android mobile device version of *Fortnite: Battle Royale*, it was around the same time that Samsung released its Galaxy Note9 smartphone and Galaxy Tab S4 tablet. To celebrate this, Epic Games offered an exclusive Galaxy outfit to people who purchased one of Samsung's new Android-based mobile devices. Details about the promotion can be found here: www.samsung.com/us/mobile/galaxy/fortnite.

A growing number of outfits have multiple styles associated with them. However, once the outfit is acquired, you then need to complete challenges to unlock each style. As you're viewing the outfits you own within the Locker, if you're able to highlight and select the Edit Style button that appears near the top-left corner of the screen (next to the Select Outfit button), you can then select from multiple styles or determine what you need to accomplish in order to first unlock the available styles.

Show You Mean Business with Accessory Items

In addition to outfits, additional ways to customize the appearance of your soldier include using optional back bling designs, pickaxe designs, glider designs, and contrail designs. Each of these items is stored within a separate section of your Locker once they're acquired, purchased, or unlocked.

These additional items can be part of a set, but sometimes they're sold individually. Any item that's been added to your Locker, however, can be mixed and matched as you're choosing your soldier's appearance.

Before any match, from the Lobby, access the Locker. Displayed on the right is the current appearance of your soldier. On the left, you'll see the name and details for the currently selected outfit, which in this case is Ventura, which is part of the Venture set.

Look below the Account and Equipment heading. You'll see seven slots. The left-most slot is a Banner slot. Select this to design and display a personalized banner. Anyone can do this for free.

As you're looking at the main Locker screen, under the Account and Equipment heading, to the immediate right of the Banner slot is the Outfit slot (it's selected here and has a yellow frame around it). Select this to choose an outfit from all of the outfits that you've previously purchased, unlocked, or acquired.

Upon selecting the Outfit slot, your soldier's current appearance is displayed on the right, while thumbnails for all of the different outfits you currently have access to are displayed on the left. When you highlight an outfit, a preview of it is displayed on the right side of the screen.

Select the Randomizer thumbnail and the game will automatically choose a random outfit for you (from the selection available within your Locker) at the start of each match. You can manually change your soldier's appearance before each match, or select an overall look and stick with it as you go from match to match.

Using the appropriate controller (keyboard) buttons, you can zoom in or rotate the soldier to see the outfit from all sides and in more detail. When you select an outfit, that's the one your soldier will actually wear. Make your selection and return to the main Locker screen.

Once you return to the Locker screen, highlight and select the slot to the right of the Outfit slot to choose your soldier's back bling (backpack) design. When you select this slot, all of the back bling items you've purchased, unlocked, or acquired are displayed as thumbnails on the left side of the screen. Highlight and select the one you want to add to your soldier's outfit. A preview of how it'll look is displayed on the right side of the screen.

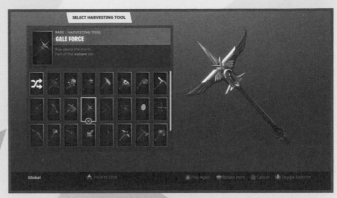

When you're actually participating in a match, all you will see is your soldier's back (and back bling) along with their pickaxe (if they're holding it, as opposed to a weapon or loot item). However, as you encounter other soldiers, the gamers controlling them will be able to see your entire outfit (along with its matching accessory items).

As you're browsing through your pickaxe designs, each time you highlight one, it will be previewed on the right side of the screen. On the left side of the screen, however, you'll see the name of the pickaxe design, as well as the name of the set it's from (if applicable). Some gamers like to dress their soldier using an outfit and accessories from the same set. Others like to make their soldier look more unique by mixing and matching outfits and items from different sets. Which option you choose is entirely up to you.

The next thing to select from the Locker is your soldier's pickaxe design. From the main Locker screen, select the pickaxe slot. Then, from the thumbnails on the left side of the screen (which showcase all of the pickaxes you've unlocked, purchased, or acquired), choose one.

After choosing a pickaxe design, from the main Locker screen, this time select the glider slot and choose which glider design you want to associate with your soldier. There are hundreds of different glider designs you can potentially purchase, acquire, or unlock. The ones available to you will be displayed when you select the glider slot of the Locker. While all of the gliders look different, they all function exactly the same way.

Gliders are used at the start of the match to help your soldier land safely after leaping from the Battle Bus. After stepping on a Launch Pad or using a Rift-to-Go item, for example, once your soldier is catapulted into the air, their glider automatically deploys to ensure a safe landing.

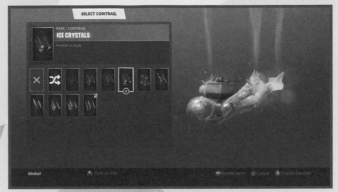

Some gliders have their own contrail design and sound effects. The contrail design that's associated with a glider cannot be selected. It's part of the glider design.

After selecting the Contrail slot from the Locker screen, choose one of the contrail thumbnails displayed to the left to see a preview of it on the right. You can then select whichever contrail design you want to link with your soldier.

During your soldier's free fall after leaping from the Battle Bus, it's possible for them to display an animated contrail design. Again, this is purely for cosmetic purposes. Contrail designs cannot be purchased separately from the Item Shop. They must be unlocked by completing challenges, or they come as part of a Twitch Prime Pack, for example. Once in a great while, a matching contrail design is included when you purchase a specific outfit, but this is rare.

The rightmost slot under the Account and Equipment heading on the Locker screen allows you to choose a Loading Screen Graphic. This is displayed as the game is loading. Loading Screen Graphics must be unlocked. They're not sold from the Item Shop.

Ready, Set, Emote

One of the ways your soldier can express personality and emotion while in the pre-deployment area before a match, or while on the island during a match, is to use emotes. These can be seen by anyone around. There are four types of emotes available within *Fortnite: Battle Royale*.

Dance Move Emotes

Dance moves are the most common types of emotes. There are hundreds of different dance moves that can be purchased from the Item Shop, one at a time. Additional dance moves can be acquired as prizes by completing challenges, or they sometimes come as part of a Twitch Prime Pack or other type of promotion.

Spray Paint Tag Emotes

Every soldier carries virtual spray paint with them and can create graffiti on any flat surface within the pre-deployment area, once individual spray paint tag designs have been unlocked or acquired. These cannot be purchased from the Item Shop. Epic Games has released many different spray paint tags. Once you unlock or acquire any of them, you can pick and choose which ones you want to use to leave your mark on the island.

Graphic Icon Emotes

Once you've unlocked this type of emote, it can be tossed into the air for everyone in the immediate area to see. There are many individual graphic icon emotes that have been released by Epic Games, but each needs to be unlocked or acquired separately. They're not sold from the Item Shop.

Specialty Emotes

As you explore the island, you'll discover a bunch of basketball courts in places like Lazy Links and Paradise Palms, although they can also be found within many other points of interest.

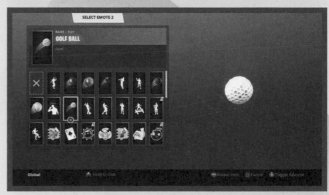

Lazy Links is also home to a rather large golf course.

There are several special emotes including a Basketball and Golf Ball that, once acquired, allow you to shoot hoops or play a round of golf while you're exploring the island. These items cannot be purchased from the Item Shop. They must be unlocked by completing challenges.

How to Use Emotes

The first step is to purchase dance moves, or unlock emotes (including dance moves, spray paint tags, graphic icons, and specialty emotes). Once you've acquired one or more types of emotes, they get stored within the Locker. Remember, for each type of emote, there are many potential designs or variations that can be purchased or unlocked.

Before a match, from the Lobby, access the Locker. On the left side of the screen, below the Emotes heading, you'll discover six slots. During any individual match, your soldier can carry and use up to six different emotes. However, each emote can be used as often as you'd like.

When using an emote during a match, your soldier will not be in Combat mode or Building mode, so they'll be momentarily vulnerable to attack. Before opting to use any emote, make

sure it's safe to do so. It's always safe, however, to use emotes while in the pre-deployment area before a match. Your soldier can't be harmed there.

One at a time, select and open an Emotes slot from the Locker screen. On the left will be thumbnails for all of the different emotes you've purchased, unlocked, or have acquired. When you highlight one, a preview of it gets displayed on the right side of the screen. When you select it, that one emote gets associated with the Emotes slot that's open.

Add a different emote to each of the six Emotes slots. This can be any combination of dance moves, spray paint tags, graphic icons, or specialty emotes.

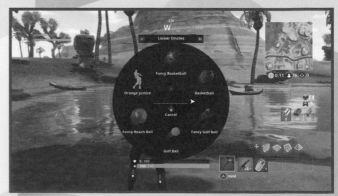

While in the pre-deployment area, or during any match, to use an emote, access this Emotes menu (by pressing the appropriate button on your controller or keyboard) and then select which of the six emotes you want to use.

It's possible to perform several different dance moves back-to-back in order to showcase some slick choreography. You're also able to use several spray paint tags at the same location to create unique and attention-getting graffiti.

How to Use Specialty Emotes

Once your soldier is positioned, access the Emotes menu and select the Basketball. Your soldier will toss the basketball in the direction he or she is facing (hopefully toward the hoop).

Anytime you come across a basketball court on the island, if your soldier is carrying a Basketball or Fancy Basketball emote within their Emotes menu, first position your soldier in front of a basketball hoop. You'll need to select the best angle and distance from the hoop to shoot from.

As the basketball soars through the air, your objective is to get it into the basket. If you're successful, you'll see some confetti and hear a celebratory sound effect, but this offers zero tactical advantage during a match. Playing basketball is purely for fun.

Of course, if there's a match going on, enemy soldiers can attack at any moment, so be prepared to quickly switch back into Combat mode or Building mode to launch counter attacks or defend your soldier. If you're playing a Duos or Squads game, you can play basketball with your partner or squad mates.

While visiting the golf course at Lazy Links (or anytime for that matter), if your soldier is carrying a Golf Ball emote, he or she can use their pickaxe as a golf club in order to play a quick round of golf. To play golf, approach a hole that is part of the golf course. Each hole is identified with a flag.

Once your soldier is in position, access the Emotes menu and select the Golf Ball or Fancy Golf Ball emote. Your soldier will then use their pickaxe to swing and hit the ball. The objective is to achieve a hole in one. You may need to reposition your soldier a few times to accomplish this.

Several different Golf Ball and Basketball designs are available as separate emotes. Add one or all of them to your soldier's Emotes menu before a match if you want to play a round of golf or shoot some hoops during a match. Don't forget, there are still enemy soldiers everywhere, so just because you want to have some fun, that doesn't mean your enemies will allow a temporary cease fire. An attack can be launched at any time.

Be on the lookout for these, and then decide if you want to add one or more of these special emotes to your soldier's emotes menu. Otherwise, they can't be used during a match.

The Beach Balls can be tossed around anywhere on the island, such as near a lake.

Periodically, Epic Games introduces other types of specialty emotes into the game, such as a Beach Ball or Fancy Beach Ball.

After customizing the appearance of your soldier and choosing which emotes will be added to their Emotes menu, return to the Lobby. Select which game play mode you want to experience, and then choose the Play option to enter into a match. This is when the fun and challenge really begins!

SECTION 3

AN "A" TO "Z" GUIDE TO 50 AWESOME *FORTNITE: BATTLE ROYALE* OUTFITS

Each day, Epic Games releases a new selection of outfits and related accessory items. Most are offered for sale from the Item Shop.

Unless you're willing to spend thousands of dollars, complete all of the game's Battle Pass challenges, and also participate in all of the promotions that involve outfit and accessory item giveaways, you'll never be able to acquire the entire collection.

Out of the hundreds of outfits thus far released, you're about to discover details about 50 of the more popular and unique ones, plus discover some useful tips and strategies to use when playing *Fortnite: Battle Royale*.

While many of the featured outfits are categorized as "Legendary," most will likely be rereleased sometime in the future, giving you a chance to acquire the ones you love if you missed them when they were first introduced. They're listed here in alphabetical order.

A

Abstrakt

SET NAME	RARITY	COST (V-BUCKS)	OPTIONAL STYLES	HOW IT'S ACQUIRED	AVAILABLE ACCESSORY ITEMS	
Aerosol Assassins	Epic	1,500	No	Item Shop	Back Bling	Tag Bag
					Pickaxe	Renegade Roller
					Glider	No
					Contrail	Spray Paint

What You Should Know . . .

Abstrakt, which is part of the Aerosol Assassins set, was introduced at the same time Epic Games introduced spray paint tags into the game (back in Season 4). Teknique is the female version of this outfit.

The matching back bling in the Aerosol Assassins set contains large canisters of colorful spray paint, and the optional pickaxe design looks like a paint roller. However, all soldiers, regardless of which outfit they're wearing, have the ability to unlock and use spray paint tags on any flat surface within the pre-deployment area or on the island itself during a match.

Gaming Tips . . .

Anytime you choose to use a spray paint tag during a match, make sure there are no enemies around. While you're creating graffiti, your soldier will not be able to use a weapon or build, plus he or she will need to be facing the wall that's being tagged.

To make a spray paint tag disappear once it's been applied, simply shoot at it, or smash it with your soldier's pickaxe. You can also simply paint over it.

B

Bandolier

SET NAME	RARITY	COST (V-BUCKS)	OPTIONAL STYLES	HOW IT'S ACQUIRED	AVAILABLE ACCESSORY ITEMS	
None	Epic	1,500	No	Item Shop	Back Bling	No
					Pickaxe	No
					Glider	No
					Contrail	No

What You Should Know . . .

This lone soldier is all muscle and meanness. You can combine this outfit with any back bling, pickaxe, glider, and contrail design.

Gaming Tips . . .

After leaping from the Battle Bus and free falling toward the island, use the navigational controls to point your soldier downward, so he or she descends faster. Ideally, you want to be the first soldier to land at your desired landing location, so you can immediately grab a weapon and protect yourself.

If you land in a location after other soldiers, chances are they'll have already grabbed the nearby weapons and ammo and will shoot you moments after you reach the island.

While your soldier's pickaxe can be used as a close-range weapon, it's very weak and no match for any type of gun or explosive weapon. If your enemy is also armed only with a pickaxe, you stand a chance of winning a fight, but you need to keep moving in between swipes with your own pickaxe to avoid getting hit by your adversary. (Some gamers refer to their pickaxe as a "harvesting tool.")

When other soldiers have reached your desired landing spot first, unless you know there's a weapon you can grab quickly, seek out an alternate landing spot.

Battle Hound

SET NAME	RARITY	COST (V-BUCKS)	OPTIONAL STYLES	HOW IT'S ACQUIRED	AVAILABLE ACCESSORY ITEMS	
Laoch	Legendary	2,000	No	Item Shop	Back Bling	Crested Cape Buckler
					Pickaxe	Silver Fang
					Glider	No
					Contrail	No

What You Should Know . . .

Part man and part beast, this outfit is sure to strike fear into your enemies when they encounter your soldier in combat. Highland Warrior is the female version of this outfit, which also has a medieval theme.

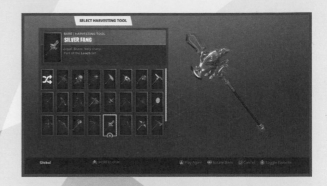

The Silver Fang is the optional pickaxe design that's part of the Laoch set.

The back bling that comes with this outfit is more of a cape than a backpack, but this is purely cosmetic. Your soldier can still hold weapons, ammo, loot items, and resources during a match.

Gaming Tips . . .

When choosing a landing location, one possible strategy is to choose a spot that's just outside of a point of interest. In other words, don't land in the middle of a popular location where you know you'll have to fight immediately. Visit a nearby structure to start building up your arsenal, and then harvest some resources before choosing to enter into a point of interest where you're guaranteed to encounter enemies.

If you're heavily armed going into a location, you'll be able to defeat enemies and collect all of the weapons, ammo, loot items, and resources they were carrying before being eliminated from the match.

Battlehawk

SET NAME	RARITY	COST (V-BUCKS)	OPTIONAL STYLES	HOW IT'S ACQUIRED	AVAILABLE ACCESSORY ITEMS	
Advanced Forces	Epic	-	No	Season 4 Battle Pass & Twitch Prime Pack 2	Back Bling	Standard Issue
					Pickaxe	Tenderizer
					Glider	No
					Contrail	No

What You Should Know . . .

In addition to Battlehawk, the Advanced Forces set includes Sledgehammer, Squad Leader, and Trailblazer. While Battlehawk could only be unlocked with the purchase of the Season 4 Battle Pass, other outfits and accessory items in this set were released in conjunction with Twitch Prime Packs.

Gaming Tips . . .

Another option when choosing a landing spot is to find a place that's extremely secluded, but that you know offers chests, as well as an abundance of weapons, ammo, and loot items lying on the ground. Once you land at one of these locations, you'll seldom encounter any enemy soldiers right away. Use the time to build up your arsenal and collect resources. As the storm expands, you'll be forced to move into closer proximity to your adversaries. By

then, you'll have a powerful arsenal at your disposal and will be fully prepared for battle.

This house with a wooden tower on top of it is located between map coordinates I2.5 and J2.5. It's just one example of a potential remote landing spot where you'll discover multiple chests plus other goodies to grab.

Land on the top of the wooden tower and smash your way down using your soldier's pickaxe to find the first one or two chests right away.

Beef Boss

SET NAME	RARITY	COST (V-BUCKS)	OPTIONAL STYLES	HOW IT'S ACQUIRED	AVAILABLE ACCESSORY ITEMS	
Durr Burger	Epic	1,500	No	Item Shop	Back Bling	Deep Fried
					Pickaxe	Patty Whacker
					Glider	Flying Saucer
					Contrail	No

What You Should Know . . .

The Beef Boss character is from Greasy Grove, home of the original Durr Burger restaurant. Every aspect of the Durr Burger set, including the outfit, back bling, pickaxe, and glider, has a fast food theme. Chances are you'll get hungry after playing a match or two with your soldier dressed in this outfit.

Gaming Tips . . .

When visiting any restaurant on the island, be sure to check behind the counter, in the kitchen, and in the bathrooms in order to find weapons, ammo, loot, and resources. The Durr Burger restaurant actually contains several levels to explore.

It's in the basement where you'll discover at least one chest, plus multiple weapons (with ammo) lying on the ground. Be the first soldier to search this area to grab what you want.

If you're playing a Duos or Squads match, and your partner or squad members are nearby, don't collect all of the weapons, ammo, and loot items you find. Leave some for your allies, so they too can build up their arsenal. However, when playing a Solo match, you want to keep your enemies from collecting weapons, ammo, loot items, or resources that could ultimately be used against you.

Because the basement of the Durr Burger restaurant contains multiple rooms, one of which is around a bend, this is a perfect place to hide and then launch a surprise attack on enemies, because they won't see you until it's too late. This is also a great location to booby trap with Traps or Remote Explosives.

Rockets are a particularly rare type of ammo, but one of the most essential when you need to use projectile explosive weapons, like a Rocket Launcher, Grenade Launcher, or Guided Missile Launcher to blow up fortresses and structures (and defeat whoever is hiding inside).

Blue Team Leader

SET NAME	RARITY	COST (V-BUCKS)	OPTIONAL STYLES	HOW IT'S ACQUIRED	AVAILABLE ACCESSORY ITEMS	
None	Rare	-	No	Exclusive to PlayStation Plus Celebration Packs	Back Bling	No
					Pickaxe	No
					Glider	Blue Streak
					Contrail	No

Collecting ammo throughout each match is essential. Many gamers don't waste time opening Ammo Boxes. This is a mistake. It's always better to stockpile ammo for all types of weapons, so you have plenty of it later when you need to fight. Take the extra few seconds and open Ammo Boxes whenever you encounter them. They're often found on shelves, under staircases, and behind objects. Sometimes, however, they're out in the open.

What You Should Know . . .

This outfit was only made available for a limited time to PlayStation Plus subscribers. However, once the outfit is added to a gamer's Locker, it can be accessed from certain other gaming systems (like the PC).

Gaming Tips . . .

Anytime your soldier needs to cross an open space, even if he or she is heavily armed, you'll need to run (don't walk) in an unpredictable, zig-zag pattern and keep jumping. This makes your soldier a moving target that's difficult for a shooter to hit.

If you're not sure where to land as you approach a specific area, while you're still airborne, check the rooftops for potential weapons and chests that are out in the open. You'll always benefit from having a weapon in hand within moments after landing on the island. However, if you spot another enemy about to land before you on the same roof, for example, seek out an alternate landing spot, since that soldier will quickly grab a weapon and shoot you (while you're still unarmed the moment you land, or potentially while you're still landing).

Brilliant Striker

SET NAME	RARITY	COST (V-BUCKS)	OPTIONAL STYLES	HOW IT'S ACQUIRED	AVAILABLE ACCESSORY ITEMS	
None	Rare	1,200	No	Item Shop	Back Bling	No
					Pickaxe	No
					Glider	No
					Contrail	No

What You Should Know . . .

You can mix and match any accessory items with the Brilliant Striker outfit since it's not part of a set.

Gaming Tips . . .

When exploring a house anywhere on the island, if there's a chest to be found, it'll likely be within the attic, garage, or basement. One way to reach the attic is to get on top of the roof from the outside, and then smash your way down using your soldier's pickaxe.

Outside of some homes you'll discover a dog house. Listen closely for the unique sound of a chest and keep your eyes peeled for a chest's golden glow. If you notice a chest hidden in a dog house, smash it once with your soldier's pickaxe and then open the chest, assuming it's safe to do so.

Sound plays an essential role in *Fortnite: Battle Royale*. To hear all of the sound effects the way they were meant to be heard (which will give you a tactical advantage), consider connecting an optional gaming headset (with a built-in microphone) to your gaming system. At the very least, plug good-quality headphones into your system. A gaming headset, however, will allow you to talk to your partner or squad mates when playing a Duos, Squads, or some types of 50 v 50 matches, for example.

Brite Bomber

SET NAME	RARITY	COST (V-BUCKS)	OPTIONAL STYLES	HOW IT'S ACQUIRED	AVAILABLE ACCESSORY ITEMS	
Sunshine & Rainbows	Rare	1,200	No	Item Shop	Back Bling	Brite Bag
					Pickaxe	Rainbow Smash
					Glider	Rainbow Rider
					Contrail	No

What You Should Know . . .

Add a little color to the island by sporting this rainbow-inspired outfit.

Gaming Tips . . .

When choosing a landing spot, one option is to land right in the heart of a popular point of interest. Only do this if you're a skilled fighter and you know exactly where you can grab a weapon and ammo within moments of landing. Chances are you'll encounter enemies right away. If you're not properly armed, you'll find yourself eliminated from a match just seconds after you land. Ideally you want to be the first soldier to land at your desired location and be the first to grab a weapon.

Burnout

SET NAME	RARITY	COST (V-BUCKS)	OPTIONAL STYLES	HOW IT'S ACQUIRED	AVAILABLE ACCESSORY ITEMS	
RPM	Epic	1,500	No	Item Shop	Back Bling	No
					Pickaxe	Lug Axe
					Glider	Cyclone or Downshift
					Contrail	No

What You Should Know . . .

Available from the Item Shop, Burnout is the male version of this outfit, and Redline is the female version (available as part of the Season 5 Battle Pass).

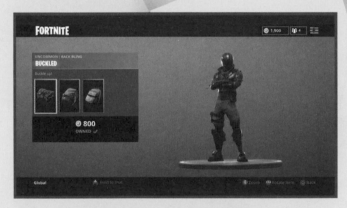

For any outfit that does not come with a matching back bling (backpack) design, you can simply use any back bling design from another set. Epic Games also occasionally offers bundles of back bling designs for a single price. Shown here is the Buckled set, which includes three back bling items that can be used with any outfit.

Of course, you can simply forgo adding a back bling design altogether. Your soldier will still be able to carry all of the necessary weapons, ammo, loot items, and resources during a match.

Gaming Tips . . .

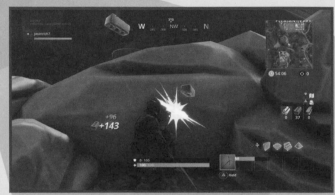

A soldier's pickaxe is a valuable tool for harvesting resources and smashing objects. Virtually any item or object you discover on the island can be smashed with a pickaxe. If it's made of wood, your soldier will harvest wood. If it's made of stone or brick, your soldier will harvest brick. Items or structures made of metal will generate metal when smashed. These resources are used for building but can also be used to acquire items from a Vending Machine. Smashing stone piles is a great way to harvest a bunch of stone.

Your soldier can store up to 1,000 wood, 1,000 stone, and 1,000 metal within the resources section of their backpack at any given time. Smashing any type of vehicle allows you to harvest metal. Anytime you smash a car, however, its security alarm will go off and make a lot of noise. If enemies are in the area, they'll be able to easily determine your location based on the noise you create.

Smashing kitchen appliances within a home, or any type of metal machinery within a factory or junkyard, is another great source of metal. When it comes to building structures and fortresses, metal is the strongest material to build with, but it takes the longest.

C

Carbide

SET NAME	RARITY	COST (V-BUCKS)	OPTIONAL STYLES	HOW IT'S ACQUIRED	AVAILABLE ACCESSORY ITEMS	
Carbide	Legendary	-	Yes	Season 4 Battle Pass	Back Bling	No
					Pickaxe	Positron
					Glider	Intrepid
					Contrail	No

What You Should Know . . .

Carbide is one of the first outfits to offer additional styles that must be unlocked by completing challenges. There are ten different style items that can be unlocked.

Once the styles are unlocked, mix and match them to give your soldier a customized look that shows off your accomplishments related to completing the required style challenges.

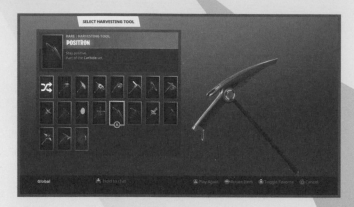

The Positron is the pickaxe design that goes with this outfit.

Gaming Tips . . .

Any type of shotgun is one of the most versatile weapons available. It can be used at close range or mid range with good accuracy, but it can also be used as a long-range weapon in a pinch. However, as you get farther away from your target, the aiming accuracy and strength of a shotgun weapon diminishes.

When shooting any type of gun, your aim will improve if your soldier is standing still. Accuracy improves even more if your soldier is crouching down. You'll have the most difficulty accurately targeting your weapon if your soldier is running or jumping at the same time he or she is shooting.

Keep an eye on the size of the weapon's targeting crosshairs while you're shooting. The smaller the crosshair becomes, the more accurate your aim will be. Moving, holding down the trigger, and/or jumping while shooting all cause the crosshairs to become larger, which decreases your aim and shooting accuracy.

While you're inside of a house, work on building up your resource stockpile by smashing furniture, objects, and even the walls. Every so often, however, stop what you're doing and listen for enemies who may be nearby. Using your pickaxe to smash objects creates noise. You don't want an enemy to be able to sneak up on you and attack because you didn't hear them approaching.

Chomp Sr. is one of the more whimsical outfits ever offered. You guessed it, the outfit and all of its optional accessory items have a shark theme, although your soldier will definitely do his best work when he's on land and not in water.

Chomp Sr.

SET NAME	RARITY	COST (V-BUCKS)	OPTIONAL STYLES	HOW IT'S ACQUIRED	AVAILABLE ACCESSORY ITEMS	
Chomp	Legendary	2,000	No	Item Shop	Back Bling	Shark Fin
					Pickaxe	Chomp Jr.
					Glider	Laser Chomp
					Contrail	No

Laser Chomp is the glider design that goes along with this outfit. Who would have guessed a giant shark (with a laser on its head) could soar through the air and ensure a soldier's safe landing?

What You Should Know . . .

Chomp Sr. has its own optional dance move (available separately) called the Rocket Spinner. It's very rare for emotes to be directly associated with specific outfit designs.

Gaming Tips . . .

Speaking of water, anytime your soldier needs to cross a lake, there are two approaches. The first is simply to walk through the lake. This is a slow process and it leaves your soldier out in the open and vulnerable to attack.

A much better strategy is to build a wooden bridge and then run over it in order to cross a lake. If an enemy starts shooting, quickly build a few defensive walls around yourself for protection, or run in a zig-zag pattern and keep jumping to avoid getting hit by enemy bullets. As long as you have enough resources, you can hold down the building button while you're running to quickly build a bridge as you're moving across it. This also works when building ramps.

All Terrain Karts (ATKs) can drive over bridges or ramps built by soldiers. In fact, passengers of ATKs (while playing a Duos, Squads, or 50 v 50 match, for example) can build or use a weapon while riding in an ATK. The driver can only drive, however.

What You Should Know . . .

To build from wood you'll need to first collect wood as a resource. When you chop down trees, they'll disappear once you've harvested all of their wood. When a tree gets demolished, this can be seen from a good distance away by your enemies. To avoid being detected, keep an eye on a tree's HP meter while you're smashing it with your soldier's pickaxe. When you notice the HP meter is nearly depleted, stop smashing that tree, leave it standing, and move to another tree. You'll still collect wood, but the tree won't fall. Shown here, the tree's HP meter is down to 50 out of 600. It's the perfect time to stop harvesting this particular tree.

Chromium is the name of the female outfit within the Solid Steel set.

Diecast is what the male version of the outfit is called.

Chromium

SET NAME	RARITY	COST (V-BUCKS)	OPTIONAL STYLES	HOW IT'S ACQUIRED	AVAILABLE ACCESSORY ITEMS	
Solid Steel	Rare	1,200	No	Item Shop	**Back Bling**	No
					Pickaxe	Persuader
					Glider	Solid Strider
					Contrail	No

Gaming Tips . . .

If you choose to land in the middle of Tilted Towers, try to be the first one to land on the top of the clock tower. Smash your way through the roof. Near the top of the tower, you'll discover two chests. Use your soldier's pickaxe to smash the floor and drop down a bit. You'll find another chest about halfway down the clock tower. On the ground floor of the clock tower, there will typically be at least one additional weapon (with ammo) lying on the ground waiting to be grabbed.

When your soldier's backpack gets filled up, if he or she is carrying any type of shield powerup and your soldier's Shield meter is not yet at 100, consume or use the powerup. In this case, the soldier is carrying three Small Shield Potions. Consume two of this item and then drop the third. Doing this will free up a backpack slot and make room for the Impulse Grenade.

Circuit Breaker

SET NAME	RARITY	COST (V-BUCKS)	OPTIONAL STYLES	HOW IT'S ACQUIRED	AVAILABLE ACCESSORY ITEMS	
Overclocked	Rare	1,200	No	Item Shop	Back Bling	No
					Pickaxe	Cutting Edge
					Glider	Mainframe
					Contrail	No

What You Should Know . . .

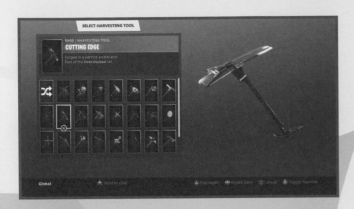

Circuit Breaker is the male version of the outfit in the Overclocked set and Cipher is the female version. Both can use the optional Cutting Edge design for their pickaxe, although any pickaxe design will work just as well.

Gaming Tips . . .

Scattered randomly throughout the island are Vending Machines. When you come across one, approach it with caution. Each allows you to purchase a random selection of weapons (with ammo) and/or loot items. Resources are used to make purchases. Here, a Suppressed Machine Gun was purchased using 150 stone.

To protect yourself and your Vending Machine purchases, consider building stone (shown here) or metal walls around yourself before making a purchase. It's a common strategy for enemies to hide and wait to ambush a soldier after they've made a purchase. When the solider at the Vending Machine is defeated, the soldier who launched the attack can collect all of the weapons, ammo, loot items, and resources the defeated soldier was carrying, including their just-purchased item from the Vending Machine.

Commando

SET NAME	RARITY	COST (V-BUCKS)	OPTIONAL STYLES	HOW IT'S ACQUIRED	AVAILABLE ACCESSORY ITEMS
None	Uncommon	800	No	Item Shop	

What You Should Know . . .

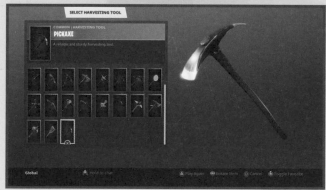

Commando is one of the Uncommon skins that can be given to new *Fortnite: Battle Royale* gamers when they first create an account and start playing. The outfit can also occasionally be purchased from the Item Shop. If this is the soldier you're given when you first start playing, you'll also receive a generic pickaxe and glider item at the same time.

Gaming Tips . . .

To reach the attic of a house while your soldier is inside it, make your way to the top floor and then build a ramp from the floor to the ceiling.

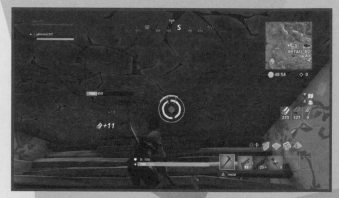

Climb the ramp and use your soldier's pickaxe to smash through the ceiling.

Locate and then open the chest you'll often (but not always) discover in the attic.

Anytime you approach the front door of a house or structure and it's already open, this means another soldier has already been inside (and could still be there). Approach with extreme caution with a weapon drawn. You can either go into the house and be prepared for a close-range firefight, or stake out the front door and be ready to launch a surprise attack as the enemy leaves.

If you suspect one or more enemies are already inside the house, tiptoe up to a window and peek inside. You can shoot at enemies through a window and surprise them. Another option is to toss a few Grenades or Clingers through an open door or window, or shoot through the opening with a Grenade Launcher, Rocket Launcher, or Guided Missile Launcher. Any of these explosive weapons will destroy part or all of the structure, and at the same time injure or defeat anyone who is inside.

Cuddle Team Leader

SET NAME	RARITY	COST (V-BUCKS)	OPTIONAL STYLES	HOW IT'S ACQUIRED	AVAILABLE ACCESSORY ITEMS	
Royale Hearts	Epic	2,000	No	Item Shop	Back Bling	Cuddle Bow
					Pickaxe	Tat Axe
					Glider	Bear Force One
					Contrail	No

What You Should Know . . .

She's bright pink, extra large, and looks like an adorable teddy bear. Cuddle Team Leader is extremely difficult to miss on the battlefield, which is one reason expert *Fortnite: Battle Royale* players don't like using this outfit. It often stands out too much. The Hearts contrail design is not necessarily part of the Royale Hearts set, but it makes a perfect addition to the overall look.

Cuddle Team Leader is the female outfit in this set, and it's become truly iconic! The male outfit in the Royale Hearts set is Love Ranger. These were two of the first outfits to get their own emotes—they're called Kiss Kiss and True Love.

The Tat Axe is Cuddle Team Leader's unique-looking pickaxe design.

Gaming Tips . . .

There are many different types of loot items to be found, collected, and used during your

stay on the island. A Slurp Juice, for example, takes just seconds to consume, but then over the next 37.5 seconds, it will boost a soldier's Health *and* Shield meters up to 75 points (about 2 points per second). If you're stuck in the storm, for example, and you have a long way to run in order to get out of it, consuming a Slurp Juice will help maintain your Health meter longer, despite the damage you're incurring from the storm. It's also a good idea to consume one of these powerups before or immediately after a battle.

Loot items can be found within chests, Supply Drops, Loot Llamas (shown here), or can sometimes be found lying on the ground, out in the open. Loot items can also be acquired by defeating an enemy and collecting the items he or she was carrying. A Loot Llama is very rare. If you encounter one, approach it with caution and then open it. You'll be rewarded with a nice collection of weapons, ammo, loot items, and resources.

What You Should Know . . .

A Chug Jug is another example of a powerup loot item. When your soldier consumes a Chug Jug, it will restore their Health and Shield meters back to 100. However, this item takes 15 seconds to consume, so make sure your soldier is somewhere safe before using it. While a Chug Jug (or any Health or Shield meter powerup) is being used or consumed, your soldier cannot move, fire a weapon, or build. In other words, they're pretty defenseless.

D

Dazzle

SET NAME	RARITY	COST (V-BUCKS)	OPTIONAL STYLES	HOW IT'S ACQUIRED	AVAILABLE ACCESSORY ITEMS	
None	Rare	1,200	No	Item Shop	Back Bling	No
					Pickaxe	No
					Glider	No
					Contrail	No

Since making its first appearance in the Item Shop, this outfit has reappeared there a bunch of times. Back in the days when Dusty Depot was a popular place on the island, Dazzle was known as "the dominator of Dusty Depot." Since then, Dusty Depot has gone through a lot of changes.

As of Season 5, it was known as Dusty Divot. Because it's located near the center of the map, almost every Battle Bus trip passes over this area (or near it), which makes it a popular landing spot. As a match progresses and the circle of safe land shrinks, the End Game portion of a match will sometimes take place near the center of the map, which forces all surviving soldiers into the area.

Gaming Tips . . .

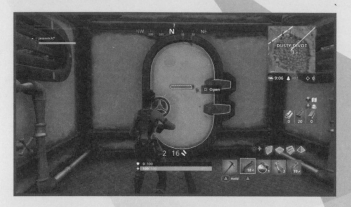

Anytime your soldier encounters a closed door, you never know what's behind it. Approach with caution and listen carefully for sounds created by potential enemies on the opposite side of the door.

Whenever you come across a large truck, be sure to check inside. You'll sometimes find a chest, or at least one or more weapons (or loot items) lying on the ground. Also, jump up or climb to the top of a truck to see if any weapons, ammo, and/or loot items can be found on its roof. These items might not be visible while standing on the ground near a truck.

Devastator

SET NAME	RARITY	COST (V-BUCKS)	OPTIONAL STYLES	HOW IT'S ACQUIRED	AVAILABLE ACCESSORY ITEMS	
Storm Fusion	Uncommon	800	No	Item Shop	Back Bling	No
					Pickaxe	Pulse Axe
					Glider	Royale X
					Contrail	No

What You Should Know . . .

Devastator is the male version of this outfit and Dominator is the female version.

Gaming Tips . . .

A Trap is one of several loot items that can be used as a weapon. Traps can be placed on a wall, floor, or ceiling within a building, structure, or fortress, for example. The trick is to place it where it can't easily be seen, so an enemy will approach and activate it. A Trap can defeat an enemy instantly. When building a fort, it's common to place one or more Traps on the inside ceiling or wall (so it's somewhat hidden) to keep enemies from easily invading.

Drift

SET NAME	RARITY	COST (V-BUCKS)	OPTIONAL STYLES	HOW IT'S ACQUIRED	AVAILABLE ACCESSORY ITEMS
Drift	Legendary	-	Yes	Battle Pass	

What You Should Know . . .

Drift is another of the first outfits to offer styles that can be unlocked by completing challenges.

To unlock this fancy robe, it's necessary to earn an additional 200,000 XP (Experience Points) while playing *Fortnite: Battle Royale*.

Gaming Tips . . .

Having a height advantage during a firefight will always work to your advantage. However, if you need to get down from somewhere high up, don't just jump! Your soldier can withstand a fall from up to three levels with little or no injury. A fall from higher up, however, can be fatal!

Instead of leaping off a steep cliff (which would cause injury or worse), slide down the edge of a cliff and you'll typically reach the ground safely.

From the top of a tall building or structure, another way to quickly reach the ground safely is to use a Launch Pad, Bouncer Pad, Rift-to-Go, or similar item that will catapult your soldier up into the air and allow you to navigate as they fall back down to land without injury.

Dynamo

SET NAME	RARITY	COST (V-BUCKS)	OPTIONAL STYLES	HOW IT'S ACQUIRED	AVAILABLE ACCESSORY ITEMS	
Lucha	Rare	1,200	No	Item Shop	Back Bling	No
					Pickaxe	Piledriver
					Glider	Libre
					Contrail	No

What You Should Know . . .

Dynamo gives off a powerful female wrestler vibe. The male version of this outfit is called Masked Fury.

Gaming Tips . . .

A Shield Potion is a powerup loot item that once consumed will activate and/or boost your soldier's Shield meter by 50 points (up to a maximum of 100). While a soldier's Health meter starts off at 100 and goes down if they get injured, the Shield meter starts at 0. It must be activated by consuming a Small Shield Potion, Shield Potion, Mushrooms, or another powerup item that works with shields.

It takes approximately 5 seconds to consume a Shield Potion, during which time your soldier cannot use a weapon, build, or move. Within one backpack slot, up to two Shield Potions can be carried and stored until they're needed. While an item is being consumed, a countdown timer showing how long it'll take is displayed near the bottom-center of the screen (directly above the Health and Shield meters on most gaming systems).

F

Fate

SET NAME	RARITY	COST (V-BUCKS)	OPTIONAL STYLES	HOW IT'S ACQUIRED	AVAILABLE ACCESSORY ITEMS	
Overseer	Legendary	2,000	No	Item Shop	Back Bling	Battle Shroud or Ominous Orb
					Pickaxe	Fated Frame
					Glider	Split Wing
					Contrail	No

What You Should Know . . .

Fate is the female version of this outfit in the Overseer set.

The Fated Frame glider design is one of the slickest-looking optional gliders available.

Omen is the male version in the Overseer set.

Gaming Tips . . .

When playing a 50 v 50 match, the island gets divided in half. The blue team (your team) gets half of the island, and the opposing red team gets the other. Each team uses a separate Battle Bus to get to the island.

During the free fall portion of a 50 v 50 match, the final circle for the match is displayed.

While your soldier is airborne, if you want to experience combat action early on, follow the white line displayed within the Location Map (shown here near the top-right corner of the screen). By following the path defined for you, you soldier will reach the circle as quickly as possible. Within the circle is ultimately where both teams will wind up for the final battles during the End Game. However, earlier in the match, this is where Supply Drops will fall.

A Semi-Automatic Sniper Rifle that's rated "Legendary" is an extremely useful long-range weapon. Once you're in the circle of a 50 v 50 match, you can hang back a bit and snipe at your enemies from a safer distance (as opposed to participating in close- or mid-range firefights). One of the great things about 50 v 50 matches is you can participate in battles with your teammates against large groups of enemies at once. These massive battles are exciting to participate in, and very different from what you experience playing a Solo, Duos, or Squads match.

Flytrap

SET NAME	RARITY	COST (V-BUCKS)	OPTIONAL STYLES	HOW IT'S ACQUIRED	AVAILABLE ACCESSORY ITEMS	
Flytrap	Legendary	2,000	No	Item Shop	Back Bling	No
					Pickaxe	Tendril
					Glider	Flytrap
					Contrail	No

What You Should Know . . .

The Flytrap outfit is part man and part plant, but 100 percent soldier.

Gaming Tips . . .

Being able to quickly build ramps is an important skill in *Fortnite: Battle Royale*. A basic wooden ramp is the fastest to create, but the weakest in terms of being able to withstand attacks. Ramps can be built anywhere. Use them to quickly get up higher than an opponent during a firefight, or to reach an otherwise inaccessible area.

One problem with really tall ramps is that they're easy for an enemy to destroy while a soldier is still on one. If this happens, the soldier climbing the ramp will fall. If it's a fall from too high up, they won't survive the plunge. To destroy a tall ramp, simply shoot at just one ramp tile located near the bottom or middle of the ramp.

Havoc

SET NAME	RARITY	COST (V-BUCKS)	OPTIONAL STYLES	HOW IT'S ACQUIRED	AVAILABLE ACCESSORY ITEMS	
None	Legendary	-	No	Amazon Twitch Prime Pack	Back Bling	No
					Pickaxe	No
					Glider	No
					Contrail	No

What You Should Know . . .

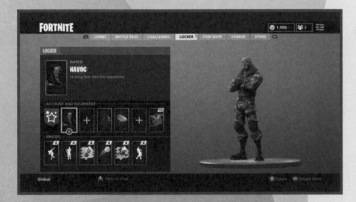

Havoc is one of the exclusive outfits that were released as part of an Amazon Twitch Prime Pack. To acquire this content, you'll need to be a paid subscriber to the Amazon Prime service and set up a free Twitch.tv account. For more information, visit www.twitch.tv/prime.

Gaming Tips . . .

If you need to build a ramp to climb up (or down) the side of a tall and steep cliff, to make it sturdier and harder to destroy, build it directly along the edge of the cliff.

This is what a standard ramp looks like. It too can be used to reach the top (or bottom) of a hill, cliff, or mountain, for example.

Huntress

SET NAME	RARITY	COST (V-BUCKS)	OPTIONAL STYLES	HOW IT'S ACQUIRED	AVAILABLE ACCESSORY ITEMS	
Norse	Epic	-	No	Battle Pass (Season 5)	Back Bling	Crested Cape
					Pickaxe	Forebearer
					Glider	Conquest
					Contrail	No

What You Should Know . . .

At the same time Epic Games introduced the Viking village (complete with a Viking ship) into the game at the start of Season 5 (it's located on top of a mountain, near map coordinates B6), male and female Viking-themed outfits with a matching pickaxe, back bling, and glider design were released. Huntress is the female outfit design.

Gaming Tips . . .

During your soldier's initial descent from the Battle Bus, you can land on top of the hill, right in the middle of the Viking village area (which is not labeled on the map).

There's also a dirt path that goes up the side of the mountain that you can follow to reach the top, or when leaving this area.

Like many unlabeled points of interest on the island map, this one contains a bunch of themed buildings in which you'll find chests, along with weapons, ammo, and loot items lying on the ground. This is also a great area to harvest resources by smashing objects and buildings with your soldier's pickaxe.

The main attraction within the Viking village is this Viking ship. Climb aboard and you'll discover useful items to grab on deck. There's typically a chest near the bow (front).

If you smash the top deck, you can drop down into the hull of the ship and find additional goodies, including a chest. Be prepared to encounter enemies while you're here!

Leviathan

SET NAME	RARITY	COST (V-BUCKS)	OPTIONAL STYLES	HOW IT'S ACQUIRED	AVAILABLE ACCESSORY ITEMS	
Space Explorers	Legendary	2,000	No	Item Shop	Back Bling	Fish Tank
					Pickaxe	Eva (or the Global Axe)
					Glider	Planetary Probe, Deep Space Lander, Voyager, or Orbital Shuttle
					Contrail	No

What You Should Know . . .

He may look like a fish in a space suit, but Leviathan is a deadly alien who's all about fighting his enemies, especially those he encounters on the mysterious island.

The other outfits in this set include Dark Voyager (available as part of the Season 3 Battle Pass), Moonwalker (available as part of the Season 3 Ballle Pass), and Dark Vanguard (available from the Item Shop).

Gaming Tips . . .

In addition to regular ramps, when you need extra protection, consider building a double ramp. This is created by building two ramps side-by-side. While this requires twice the amount of resources, your soldier can quickly leap between the two ramps, making it much more difficult for an enemy who is positioned below the ramp to figure out your soldier's location as he's climbing or descending the ramp. If one ramp gets destroyed by the enemy, your soldier can jump to the other ramp and buy themselves a few extra seconds of safety.

Another ramp-type is an over-under ramp. These too require double the resources to build, but if enemies are above your soldier, this type of ramp will offer overhead protection while he or she is climbing (or descending) the ramp. Use stone or metal for better overhead protection. This type of ramp can only be built in certain areas. To create it, position the building cursor between the upper and lower ramp, directly in front of you.

Liteshow

SET NAME	RARITY	COST (V-BUCKS)	OPTIONAL STYLES	HOW IT'S ACQUIRED	AVAILABLE ACCESSORY ITEMS	
Neon Glow	Uncommon	800	No	Item Shop	Back Bling	No
					Pickaxe	Glow Stick
					Glider	Glow Rider
					Contrail	No

What You Should Know . . .

Liteshow is the male outfit in this set.

NiteLite is the female outfit in this set.

Gaming Tips . . .

When you're outside (anywhere on the island) and one or more enemies start shooting, you can either seek out cover from a nearby structure or object or build your own structure.

One quick and easy structure to build includes just a vertical wall tile with a ramp tile built directly behind it. This simple structure will offer the most protection if it's made from metal; however, it'll take a few extra seconds for a metal structure to be constructed, during which time the tiles won't have their full defensive strength. A building tile's HP meter increases while it's being built.

Crouch down and hide behind this basic structure. An enemy will need to destroy two layers of tile walls before reaching you. For added protection from attacks coming from the side, add a vertical wall on either side

of the structure. When you're ready to shoot back, peek out the top of the ramp and shoot, then crouch back down behind the ramp for protection while your weapon is reloading, for example.

The HP Strength of Building Tiles

Every building tile you'll use to construct ramps, bridges, structures, or fortresses has its own HP meter, which determines how much damage it can withstand before getting destroyed. If you use Edit mode to add a door or window to a building tile, this often reduces the affected tile's HP strength.

In an effort to make fortress building less essential, especially during the End Game portion of a match, Epic Games has tweaked the HP strength of each shaped building tile, making wood a weaker material to build with, and stone or metal a stronger material to build with. The company will likely make additional adjustments to each tile's HP strength in the future.

As you'll discover, wood continues to be useful for quickly building ramps and bridges, but it offers minimal protection when building fortresses or structures a soldier will use for defense against attacks.

The following chart shows the HP strength of each type of building tile, based on its shape and what it's made from.

TILE SHAPE	WOOD	STONE	METAL
Horizontal Floor/ Ceiling Tile	140 HP	280 HP	460 HP
Vertical Wall Tile	150 HP	300 HP	500 HP
Ramp/Stairs Tile	140 HP	280 HP	460 HP
Pyramid-Shaped Tile	140 HP	280 HP	460 HP

Love Ranger

SET NAME	RARITY	COST (V-BUCKS)	OPTIONAL STYLES	HOW IT'S ACQUIRED	AVAILABLE ACCESSORY ITEMS	
Royale Hearts	Legendary	2,000	No	Item Shop	Back Bling	Love Wings
					Pickaxe	Tat Axe
					Glider	Bear Force One
					Contrail	No

Gaming Tips . . .

One of the quickest ways to get around the island is to drive an All Terrain Kart (ATK). These can always be found in locations in and around Paradise Palms (especially the Racetrack) and Lazy Links, but they occasionally appear in random other locations, like Tilted Towers (shown here) or Snobby Shores, for example.

What You Should Know . . .

This is the male outfit in the Royale Hearts set. It takes on the appearance of a living stone statue with wings. Love Ranger's female counterpart is the infamous Cuddle Team Leader. Both seem like they'd want to spread love across the island, but in reality, they're soldiers who are ready, willing, and able to defeat their adversaries (with your help, of course). Out of all the outfits ever released by Epic Games, Love Ranger and Cuddle Team Leader are among the most famous and iconic.

An ATK is a souped-up golf cart that can be driven across any type of terrain. If you drive over a cliff, they can even go airborne for a few seconds, and when the vehicle lands, your soldier will remain uninjured. Each ATK has its own HP meter that maxes out at 400. Each time the vehicle gets shot at or crashes into a larger object, some of its HP gets depleted. As with any other object on the island, when its HP reaches zero, it gets destroyed.

Any soldier can drive an ATK. However, while driving, they can't build or use any weapon or loot item. If an enemy starts shooting at the vehicle, the driver can either take evasive actions or quickly stop the vehicle, jump out, and start shooting back with whatever weapon they're holding. When playing a Duos, Squads, or 50 v 50 match, for example, an ATK can hold a driver plus up to three passengers. Don't forget, the passengers can shoot weapons or build simultaneously while riding in an ATK.

If a soldier jumps onto the roof of an ATK, it serves as a built-in Bouncer Pad. An ATK can drive forward or backward. There's also a brake (for stopping quickly), as well as the option to perform a Powerslide maneuver.

Powerslides can be used for making sharp turns or to force the ATK to speed up and momentarily shoot forward at a faster speed. Press the Powerslide button on the controller (or keyboard/mouse). When the wheels look like they're on fire, release the button and the ATK will shoot forward.

When you manage to flip the ATK (which is part of the fun), your soldier will need to exit the vehicle and use the Flip command to get it upright and working again.

M

Magnus

SET NAME	RARITY	COST (V-BUCKS)	OPTIONAL STYLES	HOW IT'S ACQUIRED	AVAILABLE ACCESSORY ITEMS	
Norse	Legendary	2,000	No	Item Shop	Back Bling	Enduring Cape
					Pickaxe	Forebearer
					Glider	Conquest
					Contrail	No

What You Should Know . . .

Magnus is a male Viking who's from the Viking village that's located on a hill near map coordinates B6. Huntress is the female version of the outfit.

Gaming Tips . . .

In points of interest like the Viking village (or anywhere else for that matter), when you choose to search a building, make sure you look for an attic and basement. Some structures also have a loft area (shown here), which can only be reached by building a ramp.

As you're searching a structure, if you hear the sound of a chest, but can't see it, look for a loft area. In some cases, there may be a hidden room. To reach it, use your pickaxe to smash through a wall. If you listen carefully, you should be able to determine from which direction the sound of a chest is coming. It might be above you, below you, from the side, directly in front of you, or behind you.

Surrounding the swimming pool areas in Paradise Palms and Lazy Links, you'll almost always discover one or more chests out in the open (or behind a counter, for example).

If you listen carefully, hidden chests can often be found behind walls or shrubs that you'll need to destroy in order to reach the chests.

Mission Specialist

SET NAME	RARITY	COST (V-BUCKS)	OPTIONAL STYLES	HOW IT'S ACQUIRED	AVAILABLE ACCESSORY ITEMS	
Space Explorers	Epic	-	No	Season 3 Battle Pass	Back Bling	Astro
					Pickaxe	Eva
					Glider	Orbital Shuttle, Voyager or Speed Space Lander
					Contrail	No

What You Should Know . . .

This outfit may have a spaceman theme, but when a soldier wears it on the island, he's all about combat, building, and survival! This too has become one of the more iconic outfits ever released by Epic Games.

There are several different glider designs that are part of the Space Explorers set, but each is sold separately and is only occasionally available from the Item Shop. If you want one, keep an eye out for the Orbital Shuttle or Deep Space Lander, for example.

Gaming Tips . . .

When you need to travel between the roof (or top level) of two buildings, instead of traveling to the ground, moving to the other building or structure from ground level, and then climbing back up to the roof (or a top level), build a bridge from one structure's roof to the other. This allows you to always keep your height advantage (so you can shoot down at enemies), plus it saves time.

In order to reach the roof of a house, for example, one quick option from the outside is to build a ramp from the ground to the roof. Once you're on the roof, use your soldier's pickaxe to smash downward into the attic, where you'll often find a chest.

Moisty Merman

SET NAME	RARITY	COST (V-BUCKS)	OPTIONAL STYLES	HOW IT'S ACQUIRED	AVAILABLE ACCESSORY ITEMS	
None	Legendary	2,000	No	Item Shop	Back Bling	Mertank
					Pickaxe	No
					Glider	No
					Contrail	No

What You Should Know . . .

At one time on the island, there were several movie sets that soldiers could visit. One or two might still exist, but in unlabeled points of interest. (Check near map coordinates C1.5, for example.) This outfit was inspired by the classic 1950s horror film *Creature from the Black Lagoon*.

This Mertank back bling design is provided with the Moisty Merman outfit. No other optional accessory items are available, so you can mix and match whichever pickaxe and glider design you want to use.

Gaming Tips . . .

Anytime you build a ramp or structure, if an enemy starts shooting at it, a building tile's HP meter will start to diminish. How quickly this happens will depend on the type of weapon being used, the accuracy of the shooter, and the distance the shooter is from the target. Before a building tile that's part of your ramp, bridge, structure, or fortress gets destroyed, you have the option to repair it. This requires additional resources, which you may or may not choose to use for this purpose. When a building tile has been damaged, it starts to look translucent (clear).

What You Should Know . . .

To repair a damaged building tile, face it and then press the Repair button on your controller (keyboard/mouse). The tile will start to regenerate, but the repair process will take several seconds, during which time an enemy could continue firing at the tile to cause more damage. You'll need to determine if it makes sense to repair the building or structure you're in or if it's a better idea to abandon it and/or build an alternate structure. Look for "+" icons during the repair process, which indicate repairs are being made. You'll see the tile's HP meter replenish simultaneously.

Back in the 1970s, disco was a popular type of music. In addition, wearing bright neon colors and having a mullet hairstyle was considered "cool." (What were your parents thinking?) Instead of streaming music on a smartphone from the Internet, people carried around large boom boxes that used cassette tapes. (If you don't know what a cassette tape is, Google it.) Mullet Marauder allows gamers to step into the past when it comes to their appearance.

Mullet Marauder

SET NAME	RARITY	COST (V-BUCKS)	OPTIONAL STYLES	HOW IT'S ACQUIRED	AVAILABLE ACCESSORY ITEMS	
Spandex Squad	Epic	1,500	No	Item Shop	Back Bling	Boombox
					Pickaxe	Axercise
					Glider	Windbreaker
					Contrail	No

Gaming Tips . . .

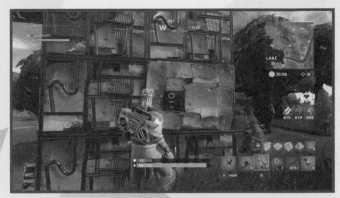

When building fortresses, many gamers forget to add a roof over their heads. If you discover this, consider rushing that fortress by building a ramp toward it, which ultimately places your soldier above the enemy fortress. As you're looking down at your enemies hiding in their roofless fortress, start shooting, drop a few Grenades, or use a Rocket Launcher or Grenade Launcher, for example. This will likely destroy the structure and defeat whoever is inside. Here, the enemy's fortress is made from stone and the ramp built by the attacking soldier is made from wood.

Anytime you have a Rocket Launcher, Grenade Launcher, or Guided Missile Launcher in your arsenal, target a building or structure from a distance. Try to shoot through the target's open window or door (or downward if there's no roof). This will allow you to do the most damage to the structure and whoever is inside.

If you're able to get close to the enemy fortress, toss a few Grenades or Clingers, for example, through an open window or door. While Clingers will stick to almost anything, Grenades will bounce off a solid object (such as a wall), which is why they need to be tossed through an open window or door.

Musha

SET NAME	RARITY	COST (V-BUCKS)	OPTIONAL STYLES	HOW IT'S ACQUIRED	AVAILABLE ACCESSORY ITEMS	
Bushido	Legendary	2,000	No	Item Shop	Back Bling	Sushimono
					Pickaxe	Cat's Claw
					Glider	Purrfect
					Contrail	No

What You Should Know . . .

The male version of this Asian-inspired outfit is Musha. The female version is Hime.

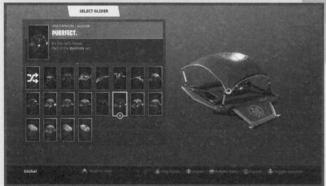

The Cat's Claw and Purrfect add to the Asian theme of this highly detailed outfit.

Gaming Tips . . .

There are many types of guns to collect during a match. For example, in the Pistol category, there are several different types of handguns (including Pistols, Suppressed Pistols, Revolvers, and Hand Canons). All serve as close-range weapons.

Each type of weapon has a rarity associated with it. This helps to determine how powerful

it is. During a match, it's common to find the same weapon multiple times, but each might have a different rarity associated with it. Weapons with a gray hue are classified as "Common."

Weapons with a green hue are rated as "Uncommon."

Weapons with a blue hue are considered "Rare," and weapons displaying a purple hue are considered "Epic."

Weapons with an orange hue are classified as "Legendary." These are the hardest to find, but they're more powerful. Each bullet shot from a Legendary weapon will cause more damage than the bullet from the same type of weapon that has a lesser rarity rating.

If you're really interested in how a weapon is rated, evaluate its DPR (Damage Per Second) rating, overall Damage Rating, Fire Rate, MAG (Magazine) Capacity, and Reload Time. This is information that Epic Games tweaks often. Select a weapon when viewing your Backpack Inventory screen to see details about it.

There are plenty of websites, including IGN. com (www.ign.com/wikis/fortnite/Weapons), Gameskinny.com (www.gameskinny.com/9mt22 /complete-fortnite-battle-royale-weapons-stats-list), and RankedBoost.com (https:// rankedboost.com/fortnite/best-weapons-ti-er-list), that provide the current stats for each weapon offered in *Fortnite: Battle Royale*, based on the latest tweaks made to the game. Just make sure when you look at this information online, it refers to the most recently released version of *Fortnite: Battle Royale*.

Noir

SET NAME	RARITY	COST (V-BUCKS)	OPTIONAL STYLES	HOW IT'S ACQUIRED	AVAILABLE ACCESSORY ITEMS	
Hardboiled	Epic	1,500	No	Item Shop	Back Bling	Cluefinder
					Pickaxe	Magnifying Axe
					Glider	Viceroy Mark 1
					Contrail	No

What You Should Know . . .

In addition to Noir, there are several other outfits that are part of the Hardboiled set, including Gumshoe (female) and Sleuth (male). Each has a private eye (detective) theme.

Gaming Tips . . .

At the same time you're building up your arsenal by collecting weapons, it's essential that you also stockpile the five different types of ammo. Without an ample supply of ammo, a weapon will be useless. Ammo types include Light Bullets (for close-range weapons, like handguns and machine guns), Medium Bullets (for most mid-range weapons, including rifles), Heavy Bullets (for sniper rifles), Shells (for shotguns), and Rockets (used by Rocket Launchers, Grenade Launchers, and Guided Missile Launchers).

Ammo can also be collected from Ammo Boxes, chests, Loot Llamas, Supply Drops, and by defeating enemies. It's important to stockpile ammo, even for weapons your soldier doesn't yet possess. Rocket ammo is often scarce, but almost always needed during the End Game, so you should grab it whenever you can.

Sometimes, ammo can be found lying on the ground, out in the open—either with or without a compatible weapon.

To see how much ammo your soldier is carrying, access the Backpack Inventory screen. Highlight and select one of the ammo icons to learn more about that type of ammo.

O

Oblivion

SET NAME	RARITY	COST (V-BUCKS)	OPTIONAL STYLES	HOW IT'S ACQUIRED	AVAILABLE ACCESSORY ITEMS	
Oblivion	Legendary	2,000	No	Item Shop	Back Bling	Destabilizer
					Pickaxe	No
					Glider	Terminus
					Contrail	No

What You Should Know . . .

Oblivion is one of the more sinister-looking outfits ever released.

The Oblivion outfit goes well with the Oracle Axe pickaxe design, although it's not technically part of the Oblivion set.

Gaming Tips . . .

One type of powerup loot item that you may come across on the island is a Cozy Campfire. A Cozy Campfire must be activated on a flat surface. Consider building a wooden floor tile and then placing the Cozy Campfire on top of it. For added safety, build stone or metal walls around yourself before activating this item.

Once activated, the flame lasts for 25 seconds. For every second one or more soldiers stand near the flame, their Health meter goes up by 2 points. Place and activate two Cozy Campfires next to each other to double the health-replenishing power.

Make sure your soldier is in a safe and secluded place before activating a Cozy Campfire. While it's being used, your soldier will not be able to move, fire a weapon, or build, so plan accordingly. One option is to build a Port-a-Fort, fill in the gap near the top with a floor tile, and then place the Cozy Campfire on top of it.

Omen

SET NAME	RARITY	COST (V-BUCKS)	OPTIONAL STYLES	HOW IT'S ACQUIRED	AVAILABLE ACCESSORY ITEMS	
Overseer	Legendary	2,000	No	Item Shop	Back Bling	Battle Shroud or Ominous Orb
					Pickaxe	Fated Frame
					Glider	Split Wing
					Contrail	No

What You Should Know . . .

Omen is the male outfit in the Overseer set, and Fate is the female version. Each has different back bling, but they use the same Fated Frame pickaxe design and Split Wing glider design. This outfit will instantly gives your soldier a powerful, mystical, and sinister appearance.

Gaming Tips . . .

A Guided Missile Launcher uses Rockets ammo and is one of the most powerful weapons

available. It can be used from a distance to accurately target enemies. However, it's even more useful for destroying structures, buildings, and fortresses. When you aim a Guided Missile Launcher, press the Aim button, place the targeting crosshairs on your target, and then pull the trigger.

While the missile is in midair, use your navigational controls to adjust its heading, to ensure a direct hit on the intended target.

As soon as the missile hits something, it'll detonate and cause a massive explosion. It's enough to take out your enemy and cause major damage to a structure, building, or fortress. The more rounds of Rockets ammo you collect, the more shots you can fire. Your enemies can see where the missile(s) are launched from, so make sure you're able to crouch down behind something to protect yourself from retaliation. You'll see the target approaching from the missile's point of view.

Overtaker

SET NAME	RARITY	COST (V-BUCKS)	OPTIONAL STYLES	HOW IT'S ACQUIRED	AVAILABLE ACCESSORY ITEMS	
Vanishing Point	Epic	1,500	No	Item Shop	Back Bling	Lane Splitter
					Pickaxe	No
					Glider	White Squall
					Contrail	No

What You Should Know . . .

Part racing car driver, part martial artist, Overtaker (and the female version of the outfit, called Whiteout) features slick-looking, black and white coloring.

The White Squall glider design looks like a futuristic flying motorcycle. It features its own contrail design and makes unique sound effects as it soars through the air.

Gaming Tips . . .

A Port-a-Fort is a useful loot item that you can find and carry with you until it's needed. Once tossed, a large metal fortress will instantly be constructed. It will require no resources to build.

Step into the Port-a-Fort as it's being constructed and jump on the piles of tires inside to leap to the top of it. (The tires automatically come with the fortress.) To ensure enemies don't try to invade, quickly build a metal floor tile over the opening.

For added protection at the top of the Port-a-Fort, build a pyramid-shaped tile (made of metal) over the metal floor tile.

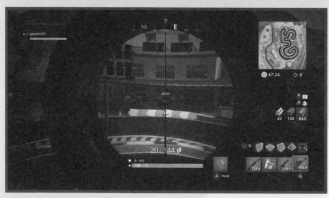

From the top of the Port-a-Fort, you'll have a 360-degree view of the surrounding area when your soldier peeks out over the fort's top edges. If you have a sniper rifle, use it to target and shoot enemies that are off in the distance.

When activated, the scope of a sniper rifle can be used as binoculars to spy on your enemies from far away, even if you don't want to use this weapon to shoot at your enemies. Use this to your tactical advantage to keep tabs on the location of your enemies. Especially during the final minutes of an End Game, it's essential that you know where your final few enemies are located at all times.

P

P.A.N.D.A. Team Leader

SET NAME	RARITY	COST (V-BUCKS)	OPTIONAL STYLES	HOW IT'S ACQUIRED	AVAILABLE ACCESSORY ITEMS	
None	Legendary	2,000	No	Item Shop	Back Bling	Bamboo
					Pickaxe	No
					Glider	No
					Contrail	No

What You Should Know . . .

Similar to the iconic Cuddle Team Leader and Fireworks Team Leader outfits, this one has an adorable panda bear theme and is a bit larger than most outfits. Epic Games has designed *Fortnite: Battle Royale* so wearing a larger skin does not make you an easier target to hit. However, wearing a larger skin does make you stand out more from a visual standpoint.

Gaming Tips . . .

As you explore the island, expect the unusual. These giant head-shaped rock statues are an example of strange things you'll encounter. These can be smashed with a pickaxe to collect a bunch of stone. However, as you get closer, you'll almost always spot two (often three) chests tucked away near the bottom of these statues. There are several strange-shaped objects and towers on the island, so even if these head statues get vaulted, there are still others to check out.

When an item gets "vaulted," this means that Epic Games has removed it from the game. However, vaulted items can be re-introduced at any time in the future. Some loot items, like Jetpacks, have been introduced, vaulted, re-introduced, and then vaulted again. From week to week, you never know what will be introduced or vaulted from the game. This is

one aspect of *Fortnite: Battle Royale* that keeps the game fresh and interesting.

Speaking of odd phenomena, here you can see a Loot Llama stuck on the side of a cliff. If enemies are nearby, approaching it will be a challenge. Assuming it's safe, however, as soon as you break apart the Loot Llama, its contents will slide down the hill and spread out.

To avoid this, build one wooden floor tile below the Loot Llama to catch its contents. If you fear an enemy attack, also build stone or metal walls around yourself before opening the Loot Llama. For protection from above, add a flat floor tile or pyramid-shaped tile overhead as a roof.

R

Rabbit Raider

SET NAME	RARITY	COST (V-BUCKS)	OPTIONAL STYLES	HOW IT'S ACQUIRED	AVAILABLE ACCESSORY ITEMS	
Pastel Patrol	Epic	1,500	No	Item Shop	Back Bling	Hard Boiled
					Pickaxe	No
					Glider	No
					Contrail	No

What You Should Know . . .

Celebrate Easter any time of the year by showing off this oversized bright pink outfit. From a distance, you'll look cute and cuddly, but from up close, an enemy will see the evil-looking mask and weapons you're holding and know you're not so friendly. The female version of this outfit is called Bunny Brawler. The drawback to wearing an oversized bright-colored outfit is that it stands out and can be seen from a distance. It might attract unwanted attention during battles.

Throughout each year, Epic Games releases (or rereleases) holiday-themed outfits and accessory items. Fireworks Team Leader was released in conjunction with the Fourth of July holiday, and several Christmas-themed outfits have been released in the past. These have become instant holiday classics.

Gaming Tips . . .

As you're exploring a house, if you think an enemy is nearby (because you hear footsteps or the opening or closing of a door), find a room to hide in, enter, and then close the door behind you. Put your back to a wall and crouch down behind an object. Aim your weapon toward the closed door. (Because the door is closed, many gamers will assume nobody has been in the room you're in and will enter.) As soon as the door is opened and you see the enemy, start shooting! When choosing where to crouch down, make sure you can't be spotted or shot at through an open window.

Throughout the island, as you're traveling between labeled points of interest on the map, you'll often encounter random buildings and structures. These are typically worth entering and exploring. In the smaller structure shown here, for example, if you look closely, from a distance you can see the glow of a chest through the holes in the roof.

If you have the time and the storm is not closing in too quickly, when exploring the random houses and structures located in between points of interest, use your soldier's pickaxe to smash objects and harvest resources. Here, for example, there's a metal car, wooden trailer, and all sorts of items in the two houses that'll allow you to stock up on wood, stone, and metal. Of course, you can (and should) also smash the houses (or structures) themselves to gather even more resources.

Approach the house. If you hear no enemy movement, build a ramp to reach the attic, smash through the wall with your pickaxe, and approach the chest to open it.

Ragnarok

SET NAME	RARITY	COST (V-BUCKS)	OPTIONAL STYLES	HOW IT'S ACQUIRED	AVAILABLE ACCESSORY ITEMS	
Harbinger	Legendary	-	Yes	Battle Pass Season 5	Back Bling	No
					Pickaxe	No
					Glider	No
					Contrail	No

What You Should Know . . .

Ragnarok was the outfit that could be unlocked by completing the 100th tier of the Battle Pass for Season 5.

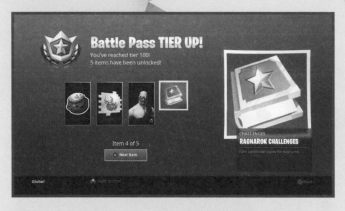

If you chose not to actually complete the challenges, there was also the option to purchase one tier at a time. Once all 100 tiers in the Season 5 Battle Pass were unlocked, the Ragnarok outfit was awarded as a prize.

Ragnarok is one of the growing selection of outfits that have unlockable styles associated

with them. In this case, there are six. To unlock them, you'll need to complete additional challenges. To determine what the challenges are, use the Edit Style option after selecting Ragnarok from the Locker, and then highlight one of the locked thumbnails. In the bottom-right corner of the screen, you'll see that to unlock the third style, you'll need to gain 75,000 Experience Points (XP). Unlike weekly or Battle Pass challenges, these outfit style-related challenges don't expire.

Gaming Tips . . .

One of the great things about being the first solider to land at a particular point of interest is that you'll discover all sorts of weapons, ammo, loot items, and resource icons lying on the ground, waiting to be grabbed. You'll also discover at least a few unopened chests.

In an area like Risky Reels, collect what you can that's out in the open, and then start searching each of the nearby buildings and structures. If someone starts shooting, crouch down behind a vehicle and shoot back.

Don't forget to check behind the movie screen (on both levels). If you're quick, you should be able to build up a really nice arsenal in less than a minute after arriving in this drive-in movie theater area.

Remember where chests and other items are located, so you'll know exactly where to return to in future matches. Chests often (but not always) spawn in the same locations match after match.

Rapscallion

SET NAME	RARITY	COST (V-BUCKS)	OPTIONAL STYLES	HOW IT'S ACQUIRED	AVAILABLE ACCESSORY ITEMS	
Jailbird	Epic	1,500	No	Item Shop	Back Bling	Burgle Bag
					Pickaxe	Nite Owl
					Glider	Starry Flight
					Contrail	No

What You Should Know . . .

Do you have a devious mind? Are you looking to get yourself into some serious trouble while exploring the island? If so, you should look the part. Choose one of the outfits in the Jailbird collection. When you wear the Rapscallion (female) or Scoundrel (male) outfit, you'll look like a criminal.

Gaming Tips . . .

There are several areas on the island that contain junk yards. In Junk Junction the junk includes tall piles of smashed vehicles. In these areas, it's best to stay as high up as possible.

Another benefit to being higher up than the car piles (by standing on a building or by building a ramp and looking down) is that you can easily spot chests and weapons that are out in the open, lying on top of the junk piles. Look carefully for the golden glow of chests.

When you're at ground level, the car piles create a maze-like area that offers no protection from above. Enemies who are higher up than you, who are standing on a building or on top of a car pile, can easily shoot down at you, because you're an easy target.

While on ground level, place a few Remote Explosives on the ground or directly on car piles. You'll see their blue lights flashing once these explosives are active.

Once they're placed, find a safe place to hide that's not too far away and that offers a clear line of sight to where you placed the explosives. As soon as you see an enemy soldier approach the area, detonate the Remote Explosives and watch them go boom!

Ravage

SET NAME	RARITY	COST (V-BUCKS)	OPTIONAL STYLES	HOW IT'S ACQUIRED	AVAILABLE ACCESSORY ITEMS	
Nevermore	Legendary	2,000	No	Item Shop	Back Bling	Dark Winds
					Pickaxe	Iron Beak
					Glider	Feathered Flyer
					Contrail	Dark Feathers

What You Should Know . . .

Ravage is another outfit that'll give your soldier a dark, sinister, and menacing appearance. This is the female version of the outfit. The male version is called Raven.

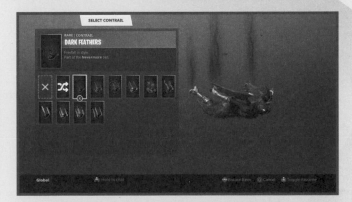

This is one of the few outfits that comes bundled with its own contrail design, called Dark Feathers.

Gaming Tips . . .

Once you've chosen your landing location after leaping from the Battle Bus, as you're descending, look for a tall building or tower to land on. Often, if you land on a tall tower, building, or silo, you'll discover chests and other useful items either on the roof or as soon as you land and smash through the roof. Upon landing on the Asian temple in the outskirts of Lucky Landing, for example, and smashing through the roof, this chest could be found and opened. It's one of several chests and Ammo Boxes available in this building.

Anytime you spot a tower structure or a smaller structure on top of a tall mountain that overlooks a popular point of interest, these are typically worthwhile places to visit. You'll find small structures or towers overlooking many popular points of interest.

If you discover a basement in a building or structure, you're virtually guaranteed to find at least one chest, assuming you're the first soldier to reach the area. Again, remember where you've found chests in previous matches. Returning to those locations is typically a smart strategy.

Not only will you often discover at least one chest, but you'll also get a bird's-eye view of the location below.

If you have one available, use a Sniper Rifle, Rocket Launcher, Grenade Launcher, or Guided Missile Launcher to pick off your enemies from a distance, since you'll have the height advantage.

Raven

SET NAME	RARITY	COST (V-BUCKS)	OPTIONAL STYLES	HOW IT'S ACQUIRED	AVAILABLE ACCESSORY ITEMS	
Nevermore	Legendary	2,000	No	Item Shop	Back Bling	Iron Cage
					Pickaxe	Iron Beak
					Glider	Feathered Flyer
					Contrail	Dark Feathers

What You Should Know . . .

This is the male outfit in the Nevermore set, and it's just as sinister and evil-looking as the Ravage (female) outfit. This one comes with a different back bling design, but shares a glider design and its own contrail design with the Ravage outfit.

Gaming Tips . . .

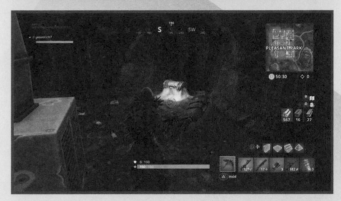

Anytime you discover a house with a cellar door on the outside, smash the door with your soldier's pickaxe, or shoot it, and then head for the basement. You'll almost always discover a chest, along with other weapons or loot items lying out in the open. If you notice a cellar door is already open when you arrive, don't bother entering. Chances are everything worthwhile has already been collected.

A Rift-to-Go is a loot item that you can find, collect, and store within your soldier's backpack until it's needed.

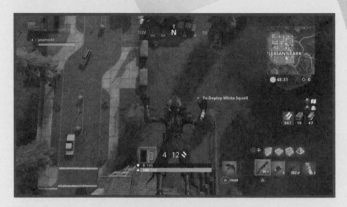

As soon as you activate a Rift-to-Go, your soldier will get caught in a rift that'll take him or her flying into the air. Their glider will automatically activate to ensure a safe landing. While airborne, however, use your navigational controls to steer your soldier and choose a landing location.

Use a Rift-to-Go to help your soldier escape from an intense battle, outrun the storm, or quickly relocate themselves to an alternate location. It can also be used to get a bird's-eye view of the surrounding area. Keep in mind, while your soldier is airborne, that he or she can be shot at, but you won't be able to shoot back.

Red Knight

SET NAME	RARITY	COST (V-BUCKS)	OPTIONAL STYLES	HOW IT'S ACQUIRED	AVAILABLE ACCESSORY ITEMS	
Fort Knights	Legendary	2,000	No	Item Shop	Back Bling	Red Shield
					Pickaxe	Crimson Axe or Axecalibur
					Glider	Sir Glide the Brave
					Contrail	No

What You Should Know . . .

Originally released way back in Season 2, Red Knight has become a popular outfit that many gamers want to add to their Locker. Several other outfits, including Black Knight (male), Royale Knight (female), and Blue Squire (male) are part of the Fort Knights set.

Each outfit in the set has its own back bling design. Shown here is the Red Shield.

Gaming Tips . . .

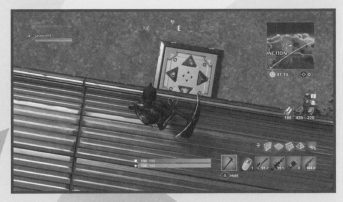

One of the loot items you may find along your journey is a Bouncer Pad. These work somewhat like Launch Pads or Rifts-to-Go, but when your soldier steps on one, he or she won't go up as high or need a glider to land safely.

If you're on ground level and want to reach the roof of a building quickly, activate a Bouncer Pad and step up it. You'll often need to build a floor tile and then place the Bouncer Pad on top of it. Step on the Bouncer Pad, and your soldier will fly into the air. As he or she is headed back toward the ground, use the navigational controls to choose their exact landing spot.

A Bouncer Pad can also be used to safely leap from the roof of a tall building or ramp back to ground level without getting injured when your soldier lands. No matter how high up your soldier goes, the landing will always be a safe one. A Bouncer Pad can be placed on any flat surface, including on a ramp. (Launch Pads cannot be placed on ramps.) With strategic placement, Bouncer Pads will help you reach otherwise inaccessible places.

Using a little creativity when it comes to Bouncer Pad placement, this item can also be used as a weapon. The goal is to get an enemy soldier trapped within a bouncing loop, which makes them vulnerable to other types of attacks while they're bouncing around uncontrollably.

Redline

SET NAME	RARITY	COST (V-BUCKS)	OPTIONAL STYLES	HOW IT'S ACQUIRED	AVAILABLE ACCESSORY ITEMS	
RPM	Epic	1,500	No	Item Shop	Back Bling	No
					Pickaxe	Lug Axe
					Glider	Cyclone or Downshift
					Contrail	No

What You Should Know . . .

Redline is the female version of the outfit in the RPM set. The male version is Cyclone.

Gaming Tips . . .

The Motel (located between map coordinates D2 and E2) is a popular location, although it's not actually labeled on the map. Over time, this area has undergone some changes, but as of Season 5, it continues to be a rundown motel, with a small office and a handful of damaged guest rooms. Search this area carefully and you'll discover many items and weapons worth collecting.

To reach the loft area in one of the guestrooms, you'll need to build a ramp. Watch for the glow of the chest.

While exploring the guestrooms, you'll need to smash away walls to find and reach everything.

The two abandoned houses located near the Motel are also worth visiting if you're looking to expand your arsenal.

S

Sun Tan Specialist

SET NAME	RARITY	COST (V-BUCKS)	OPTIONAL STYLES	HOW IT'S ACQUIRED	AVAILABLE ACCESSORY ITEMS	
Rescue Patrol	Epic	1,500	No	Item Shop	Back Bling	Rescue Ring
					Pickaxe	Rescue Paddle
					Glider	Splashdown
					Contrail	No

What You Should Know . . .

Sun Tan Specialist offers a lifeguard theme, which is fully realized when you add the optional pickaxe design and glider design. Instead of rescuing people from drowning in the water, you're more likely to find Sun Tan Specialist shooting enemies on land.

Sun Strider is the female outfit in the Rescue Patrol set.

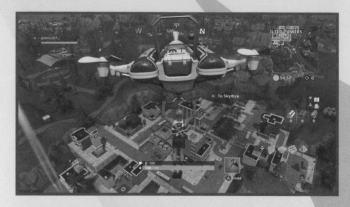

Splashdown is one of the more unique and interactive glider designs available.

Gaming Tips . . .

When it comes to building, speed is essential. To achieve speed will require a lot of practice. The styles of ramps, bridges, structures, and fortresses you're able to construct are limited only by your creativity and available resources (and of course whether or not enemies get in your way by attempting to shoot at or blow up your creations).

How to Build a 1x1 Fortress

One simple structure style you should learn to build quickly is a 1x1 fortress. It offers shielding from incoming attacks, a place to launch your own attacks from (using long-range weapons), and a location where you can heal using powerup items, as well as a way to get higher than your enemies and get a 360-degree view of your surrounding area.

Since having a height advantage and a clear line-of-sight view of your enemies who are off in the distance is important, anytime you can build on top of a hill, mountain, or even an existing structure, you'll have a bigger advantage, since it'll be harder for enemies to rush your fortress and invade.

To build a 1x1 fortress, start with one floor tile, especially if the ground is uneven or you're building on top of an existing structure. For the best protection, build this structure from stone or metal.

Stand on the newly built floor tile and add four wall tiles to surround yourself.

In the middle of the structure, add a ramp tile. As the tile is being constructed, jump on it.

You've now built the first level of the 1x1 fortress. Repeat this process as many times as you need, depending on how tall you want the fortress to be. Typically three or four levels tall is ideal.

At the top of the structure, add pyramid-shaped tiles around the four outer edges. This allows your soldier to peek out over the top and shoot from there, yet still have something to hide behind for shielding.

If you're worried about attacks from above, add an additional pyramid-shaped tile or floor/ceiling tile in the center of the structure to create a roof. Then, using Edit mode, add any windows or doors to the structure that you deem necessary.

Sushi Master

SET NAME	RARITY	COST (V-BUCKS)	OPTIONAL STYLES	HOW IT'S ACQUIRED	AVAILABLE ACCESSORY ITEMS	
Sushi	Rare	1,200	No	Item Shop	Back Bling	Chef's Choice
					Pickaxe	Filet Axe
					Glider	Flying Fish
					Contrail	No

What You Should Know . . .

Part martial artist and part sushi chef, when wearing this outfit your soldier will be able to fight or serve up a meal in a flash.

Gaming Tips . . .

One of the ongoing challenges you'll face during every match is the need to create the perfect arsenal that'll be useful in *any* situation. Realistically, this is not possible. During a mission, you'll need to swap out items and weapons you're carrying based on the challenges you anticipate facing. A lot will also depend on what weapons you're able to find and collect and which ones you're most skilled at using.

Many top-ranked gamers agree, however, that a well-rounded arsenal should include any type of rifle, any type of shotgun, a sniper rifle (with a scope), and some type of explosive weapon (either a Rocket Launcher, Grenade Launcher, Guided Missile Launcher, or explosives that can be tossed, like Grenades or Clingers), as well as a powerup loot item that can be used for healing your soldier's Health and/or Shield meter.

As you can see, this is the combination of weapons and items that the soldier has collected. Check out his backpack's inventory that's displayed in the bottom-right corner of the screen.

Of course, you can (and should) supplement your arsenal with loot items that can be used as a weapon or for healing, but that don't require a backpack slot. Traps, Bouncer Pads, and Cozy Campfires are examples of these. Ultimately, every gamer will find at least one or two weapons that they prefer and that they're skilled at using. When available, these should take priority when building your soldier's arsenal.

As you're roaming throughout the island, under trees you'll sometimes discover Apples. These are powerup items. When you pick one up and consume it, your soldier's Health meter will increase by 5 points (up to a maximum of 100 points). Apples cannot be picked up and stored in a backpack like other powerup loot items. They must be consumed when and where you find them. You'll often find a group of Apples clustered together, so if you take a minute or two, you can replenish your soldier's Health meter by 25 or more points by consuming several Apples.

Also scattered throughout the island you'll likely encounter blue Mushrooms. These work just like Apples, but each time your soldier grabs and consumes one, their Shields meter increases by 5 points (up to a maximum of 100).

When you build a ramp along the side of a hill or mountain, this makes the ramp sturdier. Normally, if an enemy shoots one tile of a ramp (near the bottom or middle), the whole ramp collapses. However, if a ramp is built along the side of a hill or mountain, individual ramp tiles can be destroyed, but the entire ramp will not fall apart. As you can see, this ramp has one tile shot out. It created a gap, but the ramp itself is still functional.

T

Tomatohead

SET NAME	RARITY	COST (V-BUCKS)	OPTIONAL STYLES	HOW IT'S ACQUIRED	AVAILABLE ACCESSORY ITEMS	
Pizza Pit	Epic	1,500	Yes	Item Shop	Back Bling	Special Delivery
					Pickaxe	Axeroni
					Glider	No
					Contrail	No

What You Should Know . . .

Out of all the outfits ever released by Epic Games within *Fortnite: Battle Royale*, perhaps the most popular and the one that everyone associates with this game is Tomatohead. At first, Tomatohead's home base was the pizza restaurant in Tomato Town, but in *Fortnite: Battle Royale*, points of interest often change.

Toward the end of Season 5, the pizza restaurant in Tomato Town was transformed into an ancient stone temple in the shape of a pyramid.

The whole area was renamed Tomato Temple. However, just like the pizza restaurant that came before it, at the top of the pyramid, a giant statue of Tomatohead's head could be seen from all around.

Tomatohead is also one of the outfits that have styles that can be unlocked by completing challenges.

Gaming Tips . . .

The temple in Tomato Temple is surprisingly large and contains many tiny, often hidden chambers that contain chests and other goodies. The trick is to explore without getting shot at by enemies.

When exploring any structure that contains smaller rooms or chambers, one option is to go inside, face the entrance, crouch down, draw your weapon, and prepare to shoot anyone who approaches, while using nearby walls or objects as cover.

In Tomato Temple, even what look like modern-day houses and structures from above will often have ancient stone ruins below them. While in this area, be prepared to engage in close-range combat, so have an appropriate weapon in hand.

Toxic Trooper

SET NAME	RARITY	COST (V-BUCKS)	OPTIONAL STYLES	HOW IT'S ACQUIRED	AVAILABLE ACCESSORY ITEMS	
Outbreak	Epic	1,500	No	Item Shop	Back Bling	Pathogen or Contagion
					Pickaxe	AutoCleave
					Glider	Meltdown
					Contrail	No

What You Should Know . . .

The male version of this outfit is called Toxic Trooper. The female version is Hazard Agent. Each has their own matching back bling design, but they share a pickaxe and glider design.

Gaming Tips . . .

Toward the end of every gaming season, strange things happen on the island. This is something you'll need to get used to.

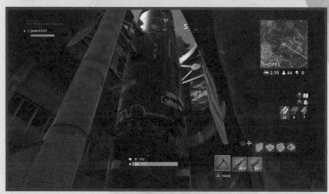

Toward the end of Season 5, what appeared to be an alien invasion took place, and this giant purple cube started appearing and moving around on the island. It temporarily created areas with reduced gravity.

At the end of Season 3, what appeared to be asteroids destroyed several areas of the island. Season 4 concluded with a nuclear missile strike that literally decimated several other points of interest. It was around this time that Toxic Trooper was added into the game to help with the radioactive cleanup.

As Season 5 started, new areas like Paradise Palms (and an entire desert area), along with Lazy Links, replaced areas that were destroyed, while other popular points of interest, like Dusty Divot, were once again revamped.

If a soldier attempted to stand on the cube, they'd be catapulted off. Trying to attack the cube resulted in lethal retaliation. Regardless of which season you're currently experiencing when playing *Fortnite: Battle Royale*, as that season winds down, expect to witness strange things happening on the island, and to encounter structures that have a mysterious purpose.

What You Should Know . . .

Speaking of unexplained mysteries on the island, throughout Season 4 and Season 5, this entrance to an underground bunker could be found within Wailing Woods (near map coordinates I3). There was no way to open this bunker door, and using weapons or explosives had no effect on it. For a long time, this structure's purpose remained a mystery!

The origins of this outfit are unknown. It seems to be inspired by superheroes and futuristic time travel. This is the male version of the outfit. It shares a pickaxe and glider design with Ventura, the female version of the outfit.

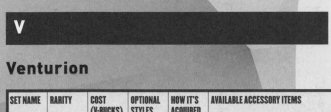

Venturion

This is the Ventura outfit.

SET NAME	RARITY	COST (V-BUCKS)	OPTIONAL STYLES	HOW IT'S ACQUIRED	AVAILABLE ACCESSORY ITEMS	
Venture	Epic	1,500	No	Item Shop	Back Bling	Venturion Cape
					Pickaxe	Airfoil
					Glider	Triumph
					Contrail	No

Gaming Tips . . .

While in the pre-deployment area or for the first few seconds your soldier is aboard the Battle Bus, check the island map. The blue line (made up of arrows) shows you the random route the bus will travel over the island and in which direction it'll travel. Use this information to help choose your landing location.

As you look at the route, keep in mind that many gamers will choose to leap from the Battle Bus at the very start of the route (in this case near Lazy Links), while others will wait until the very end (in this case near Paradise Palms). Since almost every route goes over the middle of the island, these points of interest (like Loot Lake and Tilted Towers, or whatever locations eventually replace them) will always be popular landing spots. Based on the route the bus travels, you can make an educated guess about whether or not you'll encounter a lot of enemies at a chosen landing site, and then take appropriate actions once you land.

If you land in the same location as several other soldiers, and you're not the first to arrive, your chance of getting shot and defeated within seconds after landing increases dramatically, because you won't have time to find and grab your own weapon. You'll basically be defenseless.

Regardless of where you land or what you're doing on the island, one powerup loot item that'll prove very useful is a Med Kit. This can be carried in one of your soldier's backpack slots until it's needed.

When used, it will fully replenish your soldier's Health meter back to 100. A soldier can carry up to 3 Med Kits within one backpack slot. The drawback to this item is that it takes 10 seconds to use, during which time your soldier can't use a weapon, build, or move. Make sure you choose a safe location before using a Med Kit, because your soldier will be vulnerable to attack while it's working.

Your soldier's Health meter is displayed as a green bar near the bottom-center of the screen. When active, your soldier's Shields meter is displayed as a blue bar, directly above the Health meter. If you're playing a Duos or Squads match, the Health and Shields meters for your partner or squad mates are displayed near the top-left corner of the screen, so you can see when someone gets injured and needs to be revived, or when they get defeated. The location of the Health and Shield meters may vary, based on which gaming system you're using to experience *Fortnite: Battle Royale*.

W

Wukong

SET NAME	RARITY	COST (V-BUCKS)	OPTIONAL STYLES	HOW IT'S ACQUIRED	AVAILABLE ACCESSORY ITEMS	
-	Legendary	2,000	No	Item Shop	Back Bling	Royale Flags
					Pickaxe	Jingu Bang
					Glider	No
					Contrail	No

What You Should Know . . .

This Asian-themed outfit is loosely modeled on a figure from ancient Chinese mythology known as the Monkey King. With his red, gold, and black color scheme, it's one outfit that many gamers want to add to their Locker. It periodically gets rereleased in the Item Shop, but not too often.

If you acquire the matching pickaxe design, known as Jingu Bang, you'll discover the tip of it glows after it's been used. It's more of a scepter than a traditional pickaxe, but it works just like any other pickaxe when it comes to smashing items and harvesting resources.

Gaming Tips . . .

One of the explosive loot items you have the ability to add to your arsenal is a Stink Bomb. When you toss it at a target, a cloud of toxic yellow smoke appears for 9 seconds. For every half-second an enemy gets caught in this poison cloud, it causes 5 points worth of damage to their Health or Shield meter. A soldier can hold up to 5 Stink Bombs at once in a single slot of their backpack. To create a larger and more toxic cloud, multiple Stink Bombs can be thrown at a target.

To cause the most damage using this explosive weapon, toss a few Stink Bombs into an enemy's enclosed fortress while the enemy is still inside.

If you toss a Stink Bomb at an enemy who is out in the open, he or she can easily jump or run out of the cloud, so they'll experience minimal damage.

Here, the soldier holding the Stink Bombs quickly built a wooden ramp to rush the enemy's fort from above.

As soon as he got high enough (directly over the enemy), he dropped several Stink Bombs into the heart of the fortress.

The toxic cloud quickly filled the entire enemy fortress and caused damage to whomever was inside.

Z

Zoey

SET NAME	RARITY	COST (V-BUCKS)	OPTIONAL STYLES	HOW IT'S ACQUIRED	AVAILABLE ACCESSORY ITEMS	
Sweet Tooth	Epic	1,500	No	Item Shop	Back Bling	Goodie Bag
					Pickaxe	Lollipopper
					Glider	Sugar Crash
					Contrail	No

What You Should Know . . .

Candy and bright colors were the inspiration behind the Zoey outfit. When your soldier wears it, she'll looks like a fun-loving teenager. That is, until there's a weapon in her hands. Then she becomes a threat other soldiers will need to contend with. Because of her bright pink outfit and green hair, Zoey definitely stands out on the battle field and is easy to spot. (This isn't necessarily a good thing.)

As you can see, everything about Zoey is bright, colorful, and cheerful, including the special music that plays when her Sugar Crash glider is active.

Gaming Tips . . .

Wood is the easiest resource to find and har-vest. Using your soldier's pickaxe, smash any-thing made of wood, including trees. Wooden pallets like these also generate a lot of wood.

Driving an ATK around the island is fun! It also provides a quick way to get around, especially if you need to outrun the storm. However, if you're lucky enough to find an ATK, instead of hoping in the driver's seat and driving away, consider booby-trapping it with multiple Remote Explosives.

Resource icons allow your soldier to grab a bunch of a single resource quickly. These icons are scattered throughout the island. Sometimes they're on their own, lying on the ground. They're also found within chests, Loot Llamas, and Supply Drops. When you defeat an enemy, all of the resources they had col-lected will become available to you in the form of a resource icon. In the top-right corner of the banner associated with one of these icons, it tells you how many of that resource you're about to collect.

Once these explosives are placed and active (you'll see the blue lights flashing), find some-where nearby to hide. It won't be long before an enemy approaches the ATK. As soon as the enemy hops into the driver's seat, detonate the Remote Explosives (before the soldier starts driving away). The ATK will go boom, and the enemy soldier will likely be defeated. The ATK will likely only sustain damage (some of its HP will be depleted), so it should still be drivable.

Having any type of sniper rifle in your arsenal is ideal for being able to shoot at enemies from a distance with extreme accuracy (especially if your soldier is crouched down and not moving). In a point of interest like Tilted Towers, most of a soldier's time is spent within the buildings and participating in close-range firefights.

Find a place to camp out that's on a roof or near a window. The location should have a clear line-of-sight to another building. Look for a distant window in that other building where you can see a chest inside. (You'll see the glow from a distance.) Target your sniper rifle at that chest and wait for an enemy to approach. As soon as the enemy steps into your target sights, fire!

SECTION 4

FORTNITE: BATTLE ROYALE RESOURCES

On YouTube (www.youtube.com), Twitch.TV (www.twitch.tv/directory/game/Fortnite), or Facebook Watch (www.facebook.com/watch), in the Search field, enter the search phrase *"Fortnite: Battle Royale"* to discover many game-related channels, live streams, and prerecorded videos that'll help you become a better player.

Also, be sure to check out these online resources related to *Fortnite: Battle Royale*.

WEBSITE OR YOUTUBE CHANNEL NAME	DESCRIPTION	URL
Best *Fortnite* Settings	Discover the custom game settings used by some of the world's top-rated *Fortnite: Battle Royale* players.	www.bestfortnitesettings.com
Corsair	If you're a PC gamer, consider upgrading your keyboard and mouse to ones that are designed specifically for gaming. Corsair is one of several companies that manufacturers computer keyboards, mice, and headsets specifically for gamers.	www.corsair.com
Fandom's *Fortnite* Wiki	Discover the latest news and strategies related to *Fortnite: Battle Royale*.	http://fortnite.wikia.com/wiki/Fortnite_Wiki
FantasticalGamer	A popular YouTuber who publishes *Fortnite* tutorial videos.	www.youtube.com/user/FantasticalGamer
FBR Insider	The *Fortnite: Battle Royale Insider* website offers game-related news, tips, and strategy videos.	www.fortniteinsider.com
Fortnite Config	An independent website that lists the custom game settings for dozens of top-rated *Fortnite: Battle Royale* players.	https://fortniteconfig.com
Fortnite Gamepedia Wiki	Read up-to-date descriptions of every weapon, loot item, and ammo type available within *Fortnite: Battle Royale*. This wiki also maintains a comprehensive database of soldier outfits and related items released by Epic Games.	https://fortnite.gamepedia.com/Fortnite_Wiki
Fortnite Intel	An independent source of news related to *Fortnite: Battle Royale*.	www.fortniteintel.com
Fortnite Scout	Check your personal player stats and analyze your performance using a bunch of colorful graphs and charts. Also check out the stats of other *Fortnite: Battle Royale* players.	www.fortnitescout.com

(continued on next page)

Fortnite Skins	This independent website maintains a detailed database of all *Fortnite: Battle Royale* outfits and accessory items released by Epic Games.	https://fortniteskins.net
Fortnite Stats & Leaderboard	This is an independent website that allows you to view your own *Fortnite*-related stats or discover the stats from the best players in the world.	https://fortnitestats.com
Game Informer Magazine's *Fortnite* Coverage	Discover articles, reviews, and news about *Fortnite: Battle Royale* published by *Game Informer* magazine.	www.gameinformer.com/search/searchresults.aspx?q=Fortnite
Game Skinny Online Guides	A collection of topic-specific strategy guides related to *Fortnite*.	www.gameskinny.com/tag/fortnite-guides/
GameSpot's *Fortnite* Coverage	Check out the news, reviews, and game coverage related to *Fortnite: Battle Royale* that's been published by GameSpot.	www.gamespot.com/fortnite
IGN Entertainment's *Fortnite* Coverage	Check out all IGN's past and current coverage of *Fortnite*.	www.ign.com/wikis/fortnite
Jason R. Rich's Website and Social Media Feeds	Share your *Fortnite: Battle Royale* game play strategies with this book's author and learn about his other books.	www.JasonRich.com www.FortniteGameBooks.com Twitter: @JasonRich7 Instagram: @JasonRich7
Microsoft's Xbox One *Fortnite* Website	Learn about and acquire *Fortnite: Battle Royale* if you're an Xbox One gamer.	www.microsoft.com/en-US/store/p/Fortnite-Battle-Royalee/BT5P2X999VH2
MonsterDface YouTube and Twitch.tv Channels	Watch video tutorials and live game streams from an expert *Fortnite* player.	www.youtube.com/user/MonsterdfaceLive www.Twitch.tv/MonsterDface
Ninja	Check out the live and recorded game streams from Ninja, one of the most highly skilled *Fortnite: Battle Royale* players in the world, on Twitch.tv and YouTube.	www.twitch.tv/ninja_fortnite_hyper www.youtube.com/user/NinjasHyper
Official Epic Games YouTube Channel for *Fortnite: Battle Royale*	The official *Fortnite: Battle Royale* YouTube channel.	www.youtube.com/user/epicfortnite
Pro Game Guides	This independent website maintains a detailed database of all *Fortnite: Battle Royale* outfits and accessory items released by Epic Games.	https://progameguides.com/fortnite/fortnite-features/fortnite-battle-royale-outfits-skins-cosmetics-list

ProSettings.com	An independent website that lists the custom game settings for top-ranked *Fortnite: Battle Royale* players. This website also recommends optional gaming accessories, such as keyboards, mice, graphics cards, controllers, gaming headsets, and monitors.	www.prosettings.com/game/fortnite www.prosettings.com/ best-fortnite-settings
SCUF Gaming	This company makes high-end, extremely precise, customizable wireless controllers for console-based gaming systems, including the SCUF Impact controller for the PS4. If you're looking to enhance your reaction times when playing *Fortnite: Battle Royale*, consider upgrading your wireless controller.	www.scufgaming.com
Turtle Beach Corp.	This is one of many companies that make great quality wired or wireless (Bluetooth) gaming headsets that work with all gaming platforms.	www.turtlebeach.com

Your *Fortnite: Battle Royale* Adventure Continues . . .

Fortnite: Battle Royale is an incredibly fun and challenging combat/adventure game that allows you to continuously test your gaming skills against up to 99 other gamers during each match you participate in. This is much more than just a shooting and fighting game, however.

To achieve #1 Victory Royale, in addition to mastering the use of a wide range of weapons, you'll need to take advantage of loot items, collect resources, build, avoid the storm, and utilize all sorts of survival and exploration skills as you travel around the mysterious island.

Beyond just offering high-intensity action and a real-time competitive game play experience, *Fortnite: Battle Royale* allows you to showcase your sense of style and personality by customizing the appearance of your soldier. Choosing which outfit your soldier should wear and which accessory items to use adds one more element of fun, plus a collectability aspect to the game. After all, you'll probably want to acquire outfits that are very rare or considered to be limited edition.

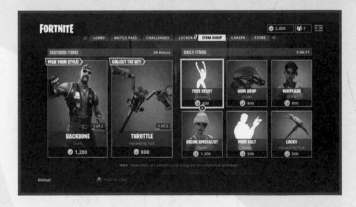

Each day, from the Item Shop, you're given a whole new opportunity to expand the contents of your Locker by acquiring outfits and matching accessory items.

When it comes to choosing the appearance of your soldier, the possibilities are truly endless, and like everything else related to *Fortnite: Battle Royale*, your options for new outfits are constantly expanding and changing. On the plus side, even if you're not an awesome, top-ranked, and highly skilled *Fortnite: Battle Royale* player, by spending some money, your soldier can still look unique and amazing!

Remember, once you start investing a lot of money by purchasing items from the Item Shop, all of which get linked to your Epic Games account, it becomes more important than ever to protect your account from hackers. Don't give out your account password to strangers, including online friends that you've never met in person and don't know in the real world.

Some of the outfits and item sets that Epic Games introduces have a specific theme. For example, Chopper and Backbone were part of the Biker Brigade set, which has a motorcycle theme.

Becoming a master when it comes to playing *Fortnite: Battle Royale* is going to take a lot of patience and practice! The most important thing, however, is to have fun playing!

As you'll quickly discover, there are literally hundreds of outfits, accessory items, and sets to choose from, including rereleases of older outfits and accessory items, plus new ones that are constantly being released. Plus, you can unlock exclusive outfits by completing Battle Pass challenges, acquiring a Twitch Prime Pack (which are released every few months), or by taking advantage of a Starter Pack promotion that Epic Games offers within the Store area of the game (where V-Bucks are purchased).